THE THUMB ON THE SCALE

Or the Supermarket Shell Game

THE THUMB

ON THE SCALE

OR THE SUPERMARKET SHELL GAME

By A. Q. Mowbray

Introduction by Marya Mannes

J. B. LIPPINCOTT COMPANY
Philadelphia and New York

340
M936

For Bev

CONTENTS

INTRODUCTION

By Marya Mannes

Those who assume that this book is mainly for the cautious housewife or the curious retailer will be doing Mr. Mowbray an injustice and themselves a disservice.

At first sight it is indeed a detailed and devastating exposure of supermarket packaging abuses and the business pressures, chicanery, and double talk which have produced and maintained them. Yet out of the long-drawn-out Congressional investigations of them led by Senator Hart of Michigan, Mr. Mowbray has added important evidence of the chilling extent to which we are a manipulated society. The manipulator in this case is not Government, which Americans have been conditioned to suspect, but the competitive free-enterprise system, which they have been schooled to trust.

As a consumer and as one of the first to testify for Senator Hart's committee six years ago, I had begun to learn the discrepancy between package and content, word and fact. Pushing a cart through the supermarket aisles, usually in haste, I had reached for the products I needed, not stopping to read the fine and often confusing print that described weight and measure because I had assumed that a quart bottle contained a quart, that a box of crackers was full, and that Economy Size meant a saving of money.

At the check-out counter I had been increasingly amazed at the money spent; at home I began to wonder why the cracker boxes had a two-inch airspace on top, why something that promised four servings was barely enough for two, and what was "new" about an old product that now cost more.

The answers have been spelled out in these pages for all to see. And what emerges is not so much a conspiracy among the manufacturers or retailers as an appalling weakening of the ethical foundation without which a democracy cannot survive. This foundation is the basis of trust between government and citizen, between seller and buyer, between producer and consumer which a free people—if they are to remain so—must voluntarily maintain. If this mutual trust is betrayed by the manipulators, the government has the duty to intervene for the manipulated, just as it is the duty of the people to intervene when Government becomes the manipulator.

"When a civilization loses its ability to discriminate between reality and illusion," writes Mr. Mowbray, "it loses the cement that binds it together, and it loses the ability to defend itself from the forces of dissolution . . . within and without." And he quotes Walter Lippmann: "If there is a dividing line between liberty and license, it is where freedom of speech is no longer respected as a procedure of truth and becomes the unrestricted right to exploit ignorance and to incite the passions of the people."

So, this book is not just about the market place. It is about the abuse of truth, whether the package is labeled "new" and means the same product in a smaller jar, or whether it is labeled "victory" and means "defeat." If we can no longer discriminate between them, as Mr. Mowbray fears, we are in real trouble.

THE THUMB ON THE SCALE

Or the Supermarket Shell Game

1

Shell Game in the Supermarket

The supermarket, glossy symbol of our affluence, is today the scene of the greatest swindle since the serpent sold Eve on the forbidden fruit. The swindler is not the giant A&P corporation, however, or Food Fair, or National Tea; nor is it the store manager or the innocent girl behind the checkout counter. The villain is the grocery package, sitting mutely on the shelf like an insidious booby trap, waiting to spring its deviltry on the unwary.

In any tour through her favorite supermarket, the housewife is surrounded by treachery. Here is a box of chocolate chip cookies only three-quarters full. Across the aisle is a jar of instant coffee marked "69 cents"; next to it is an identical jar with "7 cents off" emblazoned on the label, also marked 69 cents. Twenty feet away is a box of waxed paper containing 75 feet on the roll. Two months ago the same box contained 100 feet, and at the same price. When the manufacturer reduced the quantity, he printed the words "75 feet" in very small type on the back of the box. Who would notice that the sleight-of-hand resulted in a 33 per cent price increase?

In the next aisle are two sizes of a brand of detergent. The "regular" size is 3 pounds 3½ ounces for 69 cents. The larger "economy" size is 5 pounds 6½ ounces for $1.23. The trusting shopper fails to realize that the "economy" size costs more per ounce. She has been conditioned to assume otherwise, and the fractional weights make the calculations difficult.

In the dessert section sit two similar packaged desserts of competing brands. Both show the same net weight. One package states "4 servings," and the other, "Serves 6 to 8." On the next shelf is a beautifully wrapped package of caramels. The net weight is printed with silver ink on aluminum foil, and, unless the light strikes it just so, it is nearly invisible. Last week, the manufacturer reduced the contents from 16 to 14 ounces, but rare is the shopper who detects the shrunken pound.

And so it goes, throughout the thousands of packages on the supermarket shelves. From month to month, jars and cartons grow wider and taller to give the appearance of greater volume, while the manufacturers nibble away at the contents—an ounce here, an ounce there. Statements of net weight, required by law to appear on the package, are printed in smaller and smaller type and shifted about from one obscure corner of the package to another. The standard pound and pint disappear from the shelves, to be replaced by a profusion of fractional measures that defy calculation of price per pound, or per ounce, which is the only rational basis for cost comparisons.

The housewife is deprived of such vital information as cost, her confusion is compounded by the shrill chaos of "giant," "economy," "jumbo," and "NEW," by the anarchy of promised servings, and by the fraud of "cents-off" claims. She is adrift in a jungle, full of unseen traps, where her chances of making rational shopping decisions are very small indeed.

Unable to compare prices of competing brands, the housewife pays tribute to brand loyalty at the rate of unknown pennies per purchase. If her weekly loss is incalculable, to the food manufacturer the stakes are enormous. Americans spend more on food than on any other item in their budget. Grocery stores take in more money each year than all department, variety, and drug stores combined. Of the total retail trade of $284 billion in 1965, over $61 billion, or 21 per cent, was spent in grocery stores, and more than three quarters of that was in supermarkets.

To arrive at a figure representing the annual consumer outlay affected by the supermarket shell game, several additional factors must be considered. First, not all foods in the supermarket are part of the game. Fresh meats and produce, reasonably enough, are priced by the pound. Milk and ice cream are packaged by the pint and quart. Butter, oleomargarine, and such staples as sugar and flour are packaged by the pound. All these products, which are packaged and priced in a rational manner, comprise about 42 per cent of supermarket sales.

Second, about 8 per cent of supermarket sales are in nonfood items (soaps, detergents, waxes, polishes, paper products, etc.) that are among the worst offenders in the artful game of hoodwink-the-housewife. Finally, a substantial volume of food and other supermarket-type items are sold in other than grocery stores. Many department and variety stores, for example, have food departments.

In 1960, the Bureau of Labor Statistics made a study to determine how much money is spent by consumers to buy merchandise so packaged as to qualify as part of this shell game. The conclusion: 17 per cent of all money spent for goods and services. In 1965, Americans spent $431.5 billion for goods and services; 17 per cent of that is $73 billion. That amounts to $1,530 per family per year.

But the food and detergent and waxed paper manufacturers are not alone in having a big stake in supermarket sales. The packaging industry, which makes the cans, cartons, jars, plastic bottles, and cellophane bags, is now estimated to enjoy annual sales of nearly $15 billion. Packages consume half of all the paper and paperboard produced in this country, 95 per cent of the aluminum foil, 99 per cent of the cellophane, and 96 per cent of all the glass except flat glass. The packaging industry is the third largest user of steel, after automobiles and construction.

How much of this $15 billion annual packaging bill would be saved if the grocery manufacturer did not find it necessary to change the shape and size of his packages month by month to stay ahead in the great game of con-the-consumer? It is impossible to say. No one has attempted to estimate what proportion of packaging redesigns are for functional reasons and what proportion are dictated by the rigors of deception.

Supermarkets are gigantic business. Of the four largest retail outlets in the United States, three are supermarket chains: A&P,

Safeway, and Kroger, with a total combined annual take of more than $10 billion. In 1965 there were 158 supermarket chains with sales of $20 million or more each and combined sales of $30 billion. The six top chains—A&P, Safeway, Kroger, National Tea, Acme, and Food Fair—each grossed over $1 billion.

So let me repeat: the average family spends $1,530 per year for merchandise, mainly food in the supermarket, that is so packaged as to frustrate the normal attempt at rational shopping. If manufacturers were required to use packages that tell the truth, the whole truth, and nothing but the truth, the average family would be able to reduce its grocery bill substantially. For tests with highly educated women have shown that it is next to impossible, in the normal shopping situation, to determine the unit price (price per ounce or per pound) of these items. Thus it is impossible to compare prices between competing brands. Thus it is impossible to select the least expensive brand, should one wish to do so. And unless there is an overriding quality difference, anyone would normally wish to do so.

The lower a family's take-home pay, the larger the proportion of income that is spent for deceptively packaged supermarket wares. Thus the shell game hits hardest those who are least able to play it. For families in the lower income brackets, the saving of a dollar or two a week that might be realized if sanity were to return to grocery packaging would mean a significant improvement in living standards.

But beyond the economic harm, it is debasing and outrageous that free citizens of a free nation should be betrayed in the very act of obtaining the food to sustain their lives. It is contemptible that millions should be spent to create confusion in the marketplace. Because the food manufacturers find it more profitable to compete in artifice than in honest quality and price, the supermarket shopper is inevitably a gull and a dupe. Because the food packager finds it to his advantage to conceal the price of his goods behind shifting and expensive packaging manipulations, the housewife is deprived of the most important element in her buying decision—the price—and she wanders blindfolded through the aisles of bedlam.

Finally, chronic deception of the buyer by the seller erodes the precious mutual trust that cements the edifice of the free market. Language is prostituted, communication breaks down, mutual suspicion takes over, and free commerce is destroyed. Competition in deception can destroy the free enterprise system.

In 1961, a committee of the United States Senate began a long and frustrating attempt to enact legislation to force the food industry to restore fair play to the supermarket. For five weary years, the struggle went on, while the food industry marshalled ever stronger forces to oppose the legislation. Finally, in the fall of 1966, the battle ended in victory for the food manufacturers. Congress enacted a weakened and watered-down "Fair Packaging and Labeling Act" which is powerless to correct the most flagrant abuses. Unless new legislation can be enacted, packaging pandemonium will persist, and the American consumer will continue to pay a tithe to deception in the supermarket.

2

The Disappearing Quart

One Saturday morning, a housewife stopped her cart in the aisle of her supermarket and reached up to take a bottle of Lestoil off the shelf. Liquid detergents were a relatively new product, and this woman liked Lestoil: it was convenient to use, and it did a good cleaning job. She chose the quart jar, noting that the price had not changed since the last time she had bought a bottle. Satisfied, she put it into her cart and proceeded down the aisle.

As she trundled her cart along, she was impressed once again by the enormous variety of goods available to her. Jars, cans, cartons, bottles, and bags were heaped high on either side. The words "economy," "giant," "new," "save," and "cents off" screamed at her from brightly colored labels. She was immersed in clamoring abundance. Beneath her feeling of affluence, however, was a vague disquiet. Net weights on these gaudy packages seemed to be increasingly more difficult to find, and, when she did find them, they often made little sense. Cereal boxes were getting higher, wider, and thinner, and sometimes the air space in the top seemed exorbitant. Bottles were growing taller and acquiring a pinched waist, but she had noticed lately that she could never be sure that the "pint" bottle still held 16 ounces.

She was never sure how big a "serving" is supposed to be; usually a can that said "serves 4 to 6" was enough for two. The "cents-off" label was also confusing: she could not be sure whether the cents had been taken off before the price was stamped on the package, or whether it was to be subtracted from the stamped price. Once she had asked the clerk at the checkout counter, and he had said he didn't know; he just rang up the price stamped on the package.

Several weeks later, when the bottle of Lestoil was nearly empty, she happened to notice the words "28 fluid ounces" on the label. It took her a moment to recall that a quart was 32 ounces; then her mouth set in a firm line of resentment. Without being able to prove it—like most people, she threw away old bottles when they were empty—she was sure that the "quart" bottles of Lestoil she had bought before had truly contained a quart. Now, here was this "quart" bottle in her hand that contained only 28 ounces. And at the same price.

At the supermarket the next Saturday, she inspected all the bottles of liquid detergents on the shelves. Sure enough, all the "quart" bottles of Lestoil and of every other brand contained 28 ounces. Not only did she feel cheated, she felt helpless. What could she do about it? To change brands would be an empty gesture, since it was apparent that all the manufacturers had performed the same artful dodge.

There was one thing she could do—she could write a letter to the manufacturer and let him know how she felt about it. In a few days, she received a reply from Lestoil Products, Inc.:

> You are absolutely right. We have changed the contents of our bottles and have maintained the same size. This size is the same as competitive products, and we went to a package of similar size in order to be competitive with the giant soap companies.
> The second reason for doing this was because we felt it was better to lessen the contents rather than raise the price of our product to, say, 75 cents.
> As I am sure you realize, the soap business is a highly competitive one—perhaps, the most highly competitive in the grocery industry. When a small company such as ours attempts to compete with the "giants," we must be as competitive with them as we possibly can. We do not suggest this as an excuse for changing our package, but merely as a fact of life.

The fact of life was that keen competition among detergent

manufacturers had forced Lestoil to conceal a price increase behind a bit of packaging hocus-pocus. It was confusing. It was deceptive. And it was entirely legal.

The hidden price increase in Lestoil typifies an epidemic of packaging shenanigans that swept over the supermarket in the years following World War II. At first the unsuspecting housewife was totally duped. Out of some instinctive belief in the essential rationality of a free, competitive market, plus a faith that there were laws to protect her from thieves and pickpockets, she rarely read labels carefully. Trusting the system, fascinated and somewhat overwhelmed by the profusion of goods stacked in the bulging bins of the supermarket, harried by small children at her heels and plucking at her from the cart, hurried by swarms of shoppers on all sides, thoroughly brainwashed by incessant waves of magazine and television advertising, she bought on impulse and faith.

But a few perceptive housewives began to notice what was happening to them. They began to read the labels, to note contents, compare prices, and to remember. And they began to write letters of complaint to manufacturers and to that clearinghouse for consumer problems, Consumers Union. The following letter is typical:

Dear CU . . . Not too long ago I purchased a glass container of X brand because our current supply was dwindling. I was attracted by the bright yellow splash on the label of what I thought was the 14-ounce size we normally buy, which read "New price 25 per cent lower." When I returned home, I was immediately startled to note that the jar was smaller than the jar on our shelf, and even at a cursory glance I could see that there was less than a 25 per cent difference in the prices. A few minutes of somewhat disgusted calculation informed me that I had fallen for a baldface lie, amounting to 14 cents.

The new container held only 12 ounces instead of the usual 14 ounces and sold for 67 cents, as compared with the 83 cents I had previously paid. Without repeating my calculations, I will only state that the price, even in the deceptive, smaller container, at the advertised reduction should have been 53 cents. Knowing that prices are usually determined by the retailer according to a relatively fixed percentage, I blame the manufacturer for the lie rather than the retailer.

I cannot decide which is worse: to be cheated out of 14 cents by a glaring lie or to be subtly deceived by a change in the size of the package. Both are outrageous and certainly ought to be subject to legislative action.

In all its twenty-five-year existence, there had been no subject on which Consumers Union had received a greater volume of mail. In 1960 alone, it received some five hundred letters accusing packagers of food and other household commodities of fraud and deceit. More than a hundred different commodities were implicated, including baby food, candy, detergents, cake mixes, cookies, bread, meat, and paper products. If the letters could be believed, it appeared that the manufacturers of these commodities were engaged in a vast conspiracy to pick the pockets of the housewife.

The complaints fell into six general categories. First: the practice of slightly reducing the contents of a package (often with an accompanying redesign to give the new, smaller package the appearance of being as large as the old one), while holding the price the same or perhaps reducing it by an amount not commensurate with the reduction in contents. Second: the practice known as "slack fill." This includes various means of providing packages that are larger than their contents warrant, ranging from the simple expedient of not filling the cookie box to the top, through the cardboard tray inside the candy bar wrapper, to the more complex "dividers" of cardboard-enclosed air space inside the box of candy mints. Third: the marking of net weights in small, obscure type that makes it difficult for the shopper to determine what she is getting for her money. Fourth: the packaging of foods and detergents in odd weights that include fractional parts of a pound, or even fractional parts of an ounce, making it very difficult for the housewife to compute the cost per pound or per ounce in order to compare the cost of one brand or size with that of another. Fifth: the lavish use of such terms as "giant," "jumbo," "king size," and "economy" to describe the contents of a package, or the claim that the contents of a food package comprise a certain number of "servings." To none of these terms can any standard be applied; therefore, the complaints went, they serve to confuse the housewife and lessen the probability of her making a rational choice. Sixth and finally: the marking of a "cents-off" bargain on the package by the manufacturer, who has no control over the retail price and thus is making a promise that he has no power to keep.

The tide of complaints followed one of the most sweeping changes wrought by World War II—a revolution in the marketing of food. Before the war, the family marketing was a personal transaction between the housewife and the owner-operator of the neighborhood grocery store. Although a number of items were already packaged—canned goods, dry cereals, soap flakes, and staples such as sugar and flour—many others were sliced up, ladled out, weighed, and packaged in a plain brown paper bag by the grocery clerk under the watchful eye of the housewife. And the owner was on the premises to answer questions and receive complaints.

The end of World War II saw the rise of the supermarket and the profusion of prepackaged and "convenience" foods. Frozen foods, dehydrated "instant" foods, even whole dinners appeared on the grocer's shelves. The five or six brands of soap flakes gave way to myriad gaudy packages of the new synthetic detergents. The grocery clerk was replaced by do-it-yourself displays, the owner-operator by a harried manager for some faceless corporation. Where the typical neighborhood grocery had perhaps several hundred items on its shelves, the housewife now found herself turned loose in a cavernous, floodlit barn to wheel her cart among endless shelves holding as many as 8,000 separate items.

In 1935, there were only 300 supermarkets in the United States, with total sales of $150 million, which was an insignificant proportion of the total grocery sales in the country. Only five years later, in 1940, the number of supermarkets had grown to over 6,000, with sales of $2 billion, or nearly 24 per cent of all grocery sales. But it was in the post-war period that the supermarket really took hold. By 1965, there were over 31,000 supermarkets in the United States, with sales of nearly $45 billion, or more than 75 per cent of all grocery sales.

The revolution in the packaging and marketing of food brought many advantages. To the housewife it meant freedom from kitchen drudgery, an increase in variety in her family's diet, and, for many items, lower prices through mass distribution methods. Gone was the time when half the day was spent in preparing dinner. With a freezer and a can opener, she was emancipated.

But to the food manufacturer, the depersonalization of the supermarket brought problems. Gone was the store owner, the clerk, the salesman. Now his package sat mutely on the shelf, lost amid the profusion of its competitors, with only a few fleeting seconds to catch the eye of the passing housewife and persuade her, somehow, to buy. In the words of Ronald L. Hileman, vice-president of Jewel Tea Company:

> In self-service retailing, the package becomes the silent salesman—although some packages are not exactly silent. . . . Once on the shelf, the package must attract the consumer's attention: it must say, "Here I am; buy me."

Well and good. But the question now being asked by the housewives is: Out of how many mouths does the package speak?

3

The Package as Salesman

Once the package assumed the role of salesman, especially in the
"kitchen and bathroom" items of the supermarket, it was not long
before the competition began to shift emphasis from the contents
to the package. As Steuart Henderson Britt wrote in *The Spenders,*
"Today, most products have good quality and so must often compete on the basis of packaging. Yes, packaging can become the
discernible advantage in many instances."

In other words, one brand of soap, soup, or cigarettes is very
much like another brand of soap, soup, or cigarettes. Since it is
not possible for the manufacturer to create a "discernible advantage" in the product itself, his best bet is to create that advantage
in the package; that is, to let the package create the illusion of a
difference in the product. "It is not always the product that is best
or cheapest that is appealing," Mr. Britt continued, "but the one
that is *different* that catches our attention. Difference (or differences) in the *product* itself may be in the way it is *packaged,* or in
the *advertising and promotion* which give you an 'image' of the
product as being different. But in any case, the seller's objective is
for you to *discern* a difference, or feel that you discern a difference." (Mr. Britt's italics.)

You don't even have to discern a difference, actually; just feel
that you do. The illusion of an image will do the trick. Packaging
is no longer merely a method of holding or containing the product

for storage and shipping. It is now a major element in the advertising and promotional campaign. It is a full-fledged salesman. Indeed, its importance threatens to eclipse that of its contents. According to one sales promotion manager, "Some food processors are actually in the package business rather than the food business."

With the elevation of the package from the humdrum role of container to the infinitely more glamorous one of salesman, the psychologists, the motivationists, the hucksters, and the pitchmen rushed in to stake their claims in this new and exciting field. The profession of "packaging consultant" was born, with many applicants for the position. Anthony Oladko, vice-president for Chesebrough-Pond's Inc., wrote of the "creative and aesthetic aspects of packaging."

"This is an area," he pointed out, "which is stimulated by intense competition in the marketplace and which generates a constant succession of development, change, and upgrading in aesthetic appeal, consumer convenience, and point-of-sale impact. A considerable amount of creativity and ingenuity is required in this area. As a result, the people who are closest to the marketing function feel compelled to get into the act. It is here that we find advertising agencies; advertising managers; brand, product, and merchandising managers; consultant package designers; inside or outside directors; and, occasionally, the wives of the top executives—all feeling a sense of responsibility, assigned or otherwise, for the creation of a consumer package."

Apparently, packaging was a field in which anyone could be an expert. Not only that, it was fraught with aesthetics, and that was irresistible to the arrested Rembrandts and Shelleys who filled the ranks of the advertising agencies. Walter N. Plaut, president of Lehn & Fink Products Corporation, makers of the Tussy line of cosmetics, struck the keynote: "The major design objective of the new Tussy jars and bottles was to create a strongly emotional, feminine, visual appeal and to give this brand a youthful, wholesome image with a feeling of excitement, newness, effectiveness, and tenderness." Ordinary men might despair of expressing so much with a piece of white glass, but not Mr. Plaut:

The latest packaging redesign job took over two years to accomplish. . . . Among the first things that the team did was set down a "Design Strategy for the Tussy Staple Line" . . . to create a distinctively superior visual impression as compared to our competitors' products—an impression of optimum size, value, quality, femininity, and desirability of ownership.

[We decided that] a package must have certain characteristics, regardless of the product category:

1. It must attract attention.
2. It must immediately establish identity.
3. It must develop and hold interest.
4. It must create the desire to own the product.
5. It must compel action to purchase the product.
6. It must instill itself in the memory of the consumer.
7. It must enhance the performance, character, and total image of the brand.

Presumably the chemists working on the Tussy ointments were trying just as hard to give them optimum value as the packagers were to create an optimum "impression" of value. And presumably there is nothing wrong with a manufacturer who wishes to create an optimum "impression" of size, but it is a little unsettling to hear it said out loud.

While the cosmetic manufacturers were toiling to produce a jar that would make every girl ache to own it, the cigarette makers were aspiring to tie a man to his cigarette package as tightly as a boy clings to his dog. According to Clifford H. Goldsmith, vice-president of Philip Morris, Inc., "When the consumer buys a package of cigarettes, two things should happen: (1) he should like the package, become personally attached to it, and like it every day from there on in; and (2) he should be proud of this package when he displays it on his desk, at the dinner table, or before friends."

But the cosmetic jar and the cigarette package were only the beginning. The housewife's trip through the aisles of the supermarket was to become one grand emotional binge. The coffee jar would assuage her deep-seated loneliness, the detergent box would titillate her id, the cake-mix carton would soothe her unspeakable guilt. Even the soup can would play its part.

"Perhaps in no other segment of marketing except advertising," wrote G. E. Thomas, product marketing manager for Campbell Soup Company, "do emotions play such a significant part as they do in selecting elements that go into a package. There are established rules governing the use of color in terms of mechanics, psychology, geography, temperature, and—according to some experts—even in music, shape, odor, and taste. But we have learned through day-to-day experience that these rules are pretty abstract.

"Our selection of a package design, color combination, and typography is made on the basis of the market in which we want to be effective and the things we want the package to do. In this process some of the established rules are always violated in order to accomplish the prime objective—catching and holding the customer's attention to stimulate his desire to purchase."

Michael Keith, marketing director for W. A. Sheaffer Pen Company, put it more succinctly. The package, he said, should be "equipped with big hooks to grab the passing shopper."

As competition to make a better product had once been keen, competition to make a better package was now intense. The rush to create a package with the greatest emotional impact resulted in a whirlwind of packaging design changes. New package shapes and colors, new labels, and ever more blatant claims followed hard upon one another on the supermarket shelves.

All this is expensive. The continuous heavy costs for printing plates for labels, molds for glass and plastic bottles, dies for cardboard cartons, can be borne in only one way—increased price for the product. Steuart Britt stated that the percentage of the selling price represented by packaging "may run as much as 35 per cent for cosmetics and toiletries, 24 per cent for a great many foods, 15 per cent for wax polishes, and 5 per cent for liquor." Anthony Oladko went even higher: "In cosmetic, toiletry, and proprietary companies, the largest portion of the manufactured cost of the product is that of the packaging components. . . ." Not only was the housewife being deceived, bamboozled, and flimflammed, she was paying for the very devices that were being used to hoodwink her.

The grocery store, once a place for commerce, was now a seven-ring circus. As AFL-CIO vice-president Joseph A. Beirne put it, "If packages could shout, the uproar within the supermarket would be deafening. Packages and labels have become modern pitchmen who commonly distort or blur the truth, and who some-times resort to outright lies. Product claims have become utterly fantastic and the supermarket has been transformed into the western equivalent of the oriental bazaar."

Was all this hubbub truly a result of a vast conspiracy to confuse and cheat the housewife, or was it simply the result of an explosion of packaging technology and the rich bounty of an affluent land?

Heavy mail from readers of *Consumer Reports* complained of a decrease in contents without a compensating drop in price in a wide range of food items, ranging from cat food to candy bars. Non-food items accused of the same practice included shoe polish, writing paper, ink, clotheslines, faucet washers, patent medicines, nails, tape, thread, and so on. Disposable bags for Hoover vacuum cleaners went from a package of five bags for a dollar to four for a dollar—a 25 per cent price increase. Lint bags for clothes dryers at Sears, Roebuck jumped from four for 90 cents to three for 90 cents, in the same bag.

In 1960, Lever Brothers came out with a "new light Spry" shortening that was advertised to contain fewer calories because of a "revolutionary" process that whipped out calories. It was true. Lever Brothers had simply whipped the shortening to introduce nitrogen gas. Each cupful contained fewer calories because it contained less shortening. When it was melted and the gas removed, it was the same old Spry. The real benefit of the new promotion was to Lever Brothers: the 1-pound can now contained only 14 ounces, and the 3-pound can only 2 pounds 10 ounces.

The tea in the tea bag was diminishing. Whereas packagers had been using 5 pounds of tea to pack 1,000 bags, the weight was reduced to 4 pounds, then to 3 pounds per 1,000 bags. Few, if any, shoppers realized this; they buy tea bags by number, not by weight.

Salted peanuts had long been sold in 1-pound and ½-pound cans. The 1-pound can shrank to 15, then 14, then 13½ ounces; the ½-pound can shrank to 7, then 6¾ ounces.

In reply to complaints, some manufacturers defended the shrinking package by stating that it was in response to "consumer demand" for the smaller package. A marmalade manufacturer reduced the contents of his jar from 1 pound to 12 ounces. In answer to a letter from an irate customer, the manufacturer wrote that "a survey showed us that most customers prefer the slightly smaller size."

A letter from a cereal manufacturer to a customer who complained about his shrinking package took another tack:

> Note that today, most food products sell at 19 cents, 29 cents, 39 cents, and so forth. This is what is called a psychological price, and people will buy items at 29 cents when they won't buy at 28 cents, 38 cents, etc., even if the price is cheaper.
>
> Now, if we are going to try to price in a way that the retailer can finally come out to 29 cents or whatever, we can only put so much product into the package. In short, as a manufacturer, we begin by figuring what kind of a retail price we can get, and we work back from that point to determine what weight of product we can put in the package. Not only do we do this, but every other company in the grocery business does the same.

This letter, from one of the nation's largest manufacturers of breakfast cereals and cookies, defines precisely the practice that has come to be known as "packaging to price." The contents of the package are dictated by the retail price, and if the manufacturing cost goes up, the contents goes down. Of course, if it is a food package, the new net weight appears on the package—that is the law—but often a package redesign and the use of very small type make it less than obvious what is going on.

There were even signs that the food manufacturers were beginning to believe their own propaganda. One caramel manufacturer wrote to a complaining customer that, when costs of manufacturing went up, "we had two choices: One to reduce the net weight of the bag to correspond to the retail price we hoped to achieve, or two, to continue marketing the pound bag and increase the retail price to 42 or 43 cents. As you probably know, there has been considerable publicity connected with the increase in food prices, and we felt that our established customers would prefer . . . to have slightly fewer pieces rather than have to pay a premium and this dictated our change from 1 pound to 14 ounces." One is baffled by the mentality that could have produced the phrase "rather than have to pay a premium." Was it possible the writer could have believed that the customer would not realize that a drop in contents was a disguised increase in price? Or was the writer so involved in his deception as not to realize it himself?

Still the tide rolled on. Jars of strained baby food dropped from 5 to 4½ ounces; peanut butter from 13 to 12 ounces; shredded wheat from 12 to 10¼ ounces, in a larger box; cake mix from 1 pound 4 ounces to 1 pound 3 ounces; catsup from 14 to 12 ounces; frozen vegetables from 16 to 14, to 12, to 10, to 9 ounces; the number of paper napkins in a package fell from 80 to 60, while the number on the label sneaked around from the front to the back of the package; the soap pads in a box fell from 12 to 10, while the type size of the number on the label shrank proportionately; the 2-pound size of cottage cheese shrank to 30 ounces, in the same size carton.

Most letters to Consumers Union resented the devious nature of the changes. One noticed that the bottle of his favorite cucumber pickles had fallen from 15 to 13¾ ounces. "The small decrease was obviously small," he wrote, "so that the consumer would not notice it. I am sure we would not have noticed any decrease in net content had there been no supply of the old bottles on the shelf." "I resent and protest this rape of the public's pocketbook," fumed another writer, "though there is little I can do about it."

Little indeed. For these practices are not limited to small fly-by-night operators. As *Consumer Reports* noted, "The biggest names on supermarket shelves are among the brands most often complained about." The consumer cannot register his complaint by boycotting the offending manufacturer. As the cereal manufacturer admitted, "Not only do we do this, but every other company in the grocery business does the same."

Packaging to price is one of the two most frequent targets for consumer complaints. The other, as we have seen, is the shopper's almost complete inability to determine what he is getting for his money. Manufacturers have rendered the consumer helpless by packaging their wares in odd-size containers holding fractional pounds or ounces. This makes it all but impossible for the shopper

to calculate the price per ounce or per pound of a given product.
One box of shredded wheat weighs 11 ounces and costs 24 cents.
Its competitor weighs 10½ ounces and is priced at two for 51
cents. Who can say which is less expensive? On one day in a
supermarket in Philadelphia, the two largest manufacturers of
dry cereals had the following packages on the shelves:

Name	Weight	Price
General Mills:		
Corn Total	10½ ounces	49¢
Total	12 ounces	49¢
Wheat Stax	6½ ounces	33¢
Cheerios	7 ounces	27¢
Cheerios	10½ ounces	35¢
Cheerios	15 ounces	47¢
Wheaties	8 ounces	25¢
Wheaties	12 ounces	34¢
Wheaties	1 pound, 2 ounces	47¢
Sugar Jets	9½ ounces	34¢
Sugar Frosties	10 ounces	32¢
Lucky Charms	8 ounces	36¢
Kix	9 ounces	35¢
Trix	13 ounces	47¢
Country Corn Flakes	11½ ounces	30¢
Cocoa Puffs	9 ounces	38¢
Kellogg's:		
Rice Krispies	6 ounces	27¢
Rice Krispies	10 ounces	38¢
Rice Krispies	13 ounces	46¢
Special K	6½ ounces	28¢
Special K	10½ ounces	44¢
Corn Flakes	8 ounces	22¢
Corn Flakes	12 ounces	31¢
Corn Flakes	1 pound, 2 ounces	42¢
Pep Wheat Flakes	10 ounces	34¢
Raisin Bran	14 ounces	37¢
All-Bran	1 pound	36¢

Name	Weight		Price
Bran Buds	1	pound, 2 ounces	38¢
Sugar Smacks	10	ounces	35¢
Sugar Pops	9	ounces	35¢
Sugar Pops	12	ounces	45¢
Sugar Frosted Flakes	10	ounces	34¢
Sugar Frosted Flakes	15	ounces	47¢
Froot Loops	7	ounces	33¢
Apple Jacks	6½	ounces	37¢
Cocoa Krispies	8½	ounces	37¢

One wonders, especially after observing the generous air spaces in the tops of some of these boxes, whether the science of filling a carton with dry cereal is so exact as to necessitate the fractional part of an ounce found in a fourth of these packages. Another remarkable phenomenon is that, of the thirty-six packages, only one—the box of All-Bran—is an even pound. Three are a half pound (8 ounces). The remaining thirty-two range from 6 to 18 ounces without landing on 16.

In Washington, D.C., one shopper surveyed three supermarkets and found a total of 180 brands and sizes of detergents on the shelves. The "regular" size varied from 19 to 24½ ounces; the "large" size from 19¾ to 21¾ ounces; the "giant" size from 49 to 53½ ounces; the "king" size from 83¾ to 92 ounces; the "jumbo" size from 157 to 160 ounces; and the "home laundry" size from 257 to 320 ounces. The total inability of the average shopper to determine the price per unit weight of fractional sizes such as these makes it possible for the manufacturer to fleece the housewife in still another subtle way, as explained in the following irate letter:

In a trip on February 22 [1963] to the Grand Union store in Fairfax, Va., I examined three different sizes of Tide and noted the following circumstances:

        Small size, 1 pound, 4 ounces $0.28
        Medium size, 3 pounds, 1¼ ounces 0.73
        "Family" size, 16 pounds, 1 ounce 3.99

After spending quite a bit of time trying to decide which size was most economical, I arrived at the following results: The small size costs 1.400 cents per ounce; the medium size costs 1.482 cents per ounce; and the large size costs 1.552 cents per ounce. I have a Ph.D. in chemistry with a minor in mathematics from the University of Pittsburgh. In spite of this training, I made one mistake before arriving at the correct figures. It appears to me that the average consumer who doesn't have this type of background might have a bit more trouble trying to decide which package offered the best value.

It is obvious that on a cents-per-ounce basis these differences don't amount to much. However, on a percentage basis it works out that you pay 5 per cent more for the medium size than the small size, and 5 per cent more for the large size than the medium size.

Because of the fact that all the consumers in the country have been led to believe, through advertising practices for the last two or three generations, that it is axiomatic you get more for your money when you purchase the large package of any item, I consider such pricing to be very deceptive. The example cited is the only one which I took the trouble to analyze. This leads me to believe that the incidence of such cases must be quite large.

The writer of this letter concluded that the fractional weights of the packages had been deliberately designed to conceal the price per ounce from the consumer so that he could be deceived into paying *more per ounce* for the *largest* package. It is difficult to conceive of another explanation.

Although detergents are probably the worst offenders in this fractional numbers game, it is much too profitable a gambit for other manufacturers to ignore. To demonstrate the difficulties posed for the average housewife, Helen Nelson, consumer counsel for the State of California, organized a shopping survey. She selected five housewives, all with college training, and gave them instructions to enter a supermarket in Sacramento and buy ten items: rice (any type of white rice except precooked), solid-pack canned tomatoes, hot cereal, cheddar cheese (chunk cheddar, not sliced or grated), canned tuna fish, salt, imitation maple syrup, pancake mix, peanut butter (smooth or chunk), and liquid detergent for dishwashing by hand. They were permitted to buy any brand, any size, but they were directed to buy whichever package gave them the "largest quantity of product for the least amount of money."

The survey results showed clearly that the supermarket was corrupt. The women averaged three quarters of an hour each in their efforts to buy the least expensive items. But they still failed. On only one of the ten items did all five women succeed. On two of the items, all five shoppers failed. For the remainder of the items, the batting average was only about 50 per cent.

4

Congress to the Rescue?

As the nation entered what was hopefully dubbed the "Soaring Sixties," it was beset by many problems, from the population explosion and the "missile gap" to the Negro problem and the antics of Fidel Castro. Moreover, there was a problem which didn't make the headlines—of the some $80 billion per year that housewives were handing over at the supermarket checkout counters, a shocking percentage was being siphoned off to pay for a colossal fraud.

On June 28, 1961, the Subcommittee on Antitrust and Monopoly of the Senate Judiciary Committee began investigative hearings to determine whether new Federal legislation should be enacted to control packaging abuses. This subcommittee, under the chairmanship of Senator Estes Kefauver of Tennessee, was at that time in the midst of a battle to write a new law to protect the American consumer from dangerous and ineffective drugs. The leadership in the packaging investigation was assumed by Philip A. Hart, a forty-eight-year-old member of the subcommittee from Michigan.

Forty-one witnesses testified at the investigative hearings, held in June, October, and December, 1961. The testimony did nothing to change Hart's conviction that new legislation was needed, and on January 21, 1963, he introduced in the Senate what came to be known as the truth-in-packaging bill. After additional hearings, in March and April, 1963, the Subcommittee on Antitrust and

Monopoly approved the bill and recommended it favorably to its parent Judiciary Committee by a vote of 5 to 3. Voting for the bill were Democrats Kefauver, Hart, Thomas J. Dodd of Connecticut, and Edward V. Long of Missouri, and Republican Kenneth B. Keating of New York. Voting against the measure were Republicans Everett M. Dirksen of Illinois and Roman L. Hruska of Nebraska, and Democrat John L. McClellan of Arkansas.

It was Kefauver's last vote in the subcommittee that he had served as chairman for six years; he came from the hospital in a wheel chair to preside during the vote on the packaging bill. "We were trying very hard to get it out of the subcommittee," recalls Senator Hart, "and except for his presence in the chair, it would not have gotten out. He tugged it out." Two months later, on August 10, 1963, Kefauver died and Hart became chairman of the subcommittee.

In the Judiciary Committee, the bill faltered. As the *Wall Street Journal* noted, the Judiciary Committee was "conservative-tinged and seldom sees eye-to-eye with its antitrust subcommittee." The conservative tinge was achieved through a coalition of Republicans and Southern Democrats, and it was made fast through the chairmanship of James O. Eastland of Mississippi.

The packaging bill languished in the Judiciary Committee for the next twenty months, through both sessions of the 88th Congress. In February, 1965, with the opening of the 89th Congress, Senator Hart reintroduced his bill, and, in an effort to shake it loose and get it to the floor of the Senate, he requested that the Senate transfer jurisdiction of the bill to the more liberal Commerce Committee. A floor fight ensued, in which the bill's most powerful opponent in the Senate, Everett Dirksen, speaking in opposition to the move, chided Hart for wishing to have his own bill removed from his jurisdiction. Hart won the fight, however, and the bill was transferred.

In April and May, the Commerce Committee held its own hearings, but still the bill did not reach the floor of the Senate. Another year passed. Finally, in the spring of 1966, it was reported out of the Commerce Committee, and on June 9 it was passed by the Senate, in a somewhat weakened form, by a vote of 72 to 9.

The bill now appeared to be nearly halfway home. There remained the House of Representatives. During the late summer of 1966, the House Commerce Committee held a fourth set of hearings, accumulating an additional thousand pages of testimony, in dreary repetition of what had gone before. The House committee then proceeded to scrap the Senate bill, put together a legislative parody, slap the title "Fair Packaging and Labeling" on it, and report it to the floor of the House, where it was passed overwhelmingly on October 3, 1966, by a vote of 300 to 8.

There remained the formality of the House-Senate conference to settle differences between the House and Senate bills. But the House conferees presented the Senate with an ultimatum: it would be the House version or nothing. Reluctantly, the Senate conferees accepted the House version as better than nothing, and on November 3 President Johnson signed the bill into law.

After five years of arduous labor, the elephant had brought forth a mouse.

The law, whose ostensible purpose was to prevent "the use of unfair or deceptive methods of packaging or labeling," was itself a piece of legislative deception. Nevertheless, the congressmen hoped that everyone would be satisfied. The housewife, seeing "Packaging Bill Passed" in the headlines, would conclude that the Federal government had come to her rescue. President Johnson had his election-year consumer legislation. The food and packaging industries, which had fought the bill with every ounce of their $100-billion muscle, could breathe easily once again. Everyone had won, and everyone would get a prize.

The effort in Congress had been enormous. Most of it had been expended during the hearings held by the Antitrust and Monopoly Subcommittee in 1961, 1962, and 1963. The testimony presented at these hearings portrays the democratic process at work, and the picture that emerges is a vivid one. Rarely is an issue so easy to understand; rarely are the opposing forces so clear-cut—on one side, the voice of the consumer, pleading for the return of rationality to the marketplace; on the other, the unanimous, unremitting voice of industry, fighting to retain the status quo.

The scene of the battle was Room 2228 of the Old Senate Office

Building, which is the hearing room for the subcommittee's parent Judiciary Committee. A sweeping, semicircular dais occupies one end of the room. Embraced within the arms of the semicircle sits the witness table. Behind the witness table, and flanking it on either side, are two tables for the press, and behind these are six rows of seats for the public, with an aisle down the center.

Mahogany-paneled walls, faced with green marble from the floor to a height of four or five feet, give the room an air of somber opulence. Two massive bronze lighting fixtures hang from each wall, and around the edges of the lofty white ceiling the signs of the zodiac are embossed in recessed panels. The center of the wall behind the dais is dominated by the Great Seal of the United States, carved in mahogany.

The format for Congressional hearings is familiar to most television viewers. Members of the committee and its staff sit on the dais, the chairman in the center and the others grouped around the chairman in order of their seniority, with Republicans on one side and Democrats on the other. The witness sits at the witness table, facing the dais, with his back to the public audience.

Preliminary staff work is the key to successful hearings. The opening of hearings is usually preceded by months of preparation on the part of the committee staff, which may include lawyers, economists, and other professionals. The staff members are usually chosen by the committee (or subcommittee) chairman, who is a member of the majority party. The senior members of the minority party (during the 1960's, the Republican party) are also usually represented by staff counsel.

Dominating the hearings on the packaging bill were three figures: Senator Hart, chairman; S. Jerry Cohen, staff counsel; and Peter N. Chumbris, minority counsel representing Senator Everett Dirksen. Other members of the subcommittee and the staff drifted in and out of the hearing room from time to time, as the pressure of other work and other committee meetings permitted. But it was these three who carried the burden of the questioning.

Senator Hart, occupying the center of the dais as chairman, was a relative newcomer to the Senate in 1961. A former Detroit lawyer, he had been elected to the Senate in 1958. Before that, he had served two terms as Lieutenant Governor of Michigan. A liberal Democrat, his fairness and quiet courtesy toward witnesses earned him the respect of his opponents. One conservative Republican would later say of him: "He is a liberal with a good mind and a good balance wheel. He's not one to go hog-wild with power. He knows what he's doing, and that satisfies me."

When the hearings opened in 1961, S. Jerry Cohen, 35, had just recently joined the subcommittee staff after a term as assistant attorney general for the State of Michigan. As staff counsel for the majority, Mr. Cohen had borne much of the labor of preliminary investigations and other preparations for the hearings, and he was to play a key role in drafting the legislation. In his unruffled civility toward those who came to testify, he served well as Senator Hart's alter ego.

Minority counsel Peter N. Chumbris, whose dark good looks belied his forty-seven years, represented Senator Dirksen's interests in the hearings. A veteran of four years with the subcommittee staff, he was a somewhat more volatile spokesman for his cause than either Hart or Cohen. Perhaps one measure of his loyalty to the Senate minority leader is the fact that he named one of his sons William Dirksen Chumbris.

Day after day during these three years, while a total of eighty-eight witnesses came to offer testimony, a national question of vital economic importance narrowed down to a dialogue between the witnesses and these three men.

5

Existing Law and the Hart Bill

One of the first arguments used by opponents of the Hart bill was that existing laws were adequate to deal with the problem. In his minority view published with the subcommittee report, Senator Dirksen wrote: "Existing Federal Trade Commission and the Food and Drug Administration laws are sufficient and effective. . . . It is abundantly clear that present laws, if they are vigorously enforced, afford protection against most, if not 100 per cent, of the major complaints made at the subcommittee hearings. . . . I might add parenthetically, if existing law is as inadequate as the proponents of [the Hart bill] advocate, it means that we, the Members of Congress around this table, have been negligent for the past 15 to 25 years and that includes 8 of this Judiciary Committee."

Echoing Dirksen, Senator Hruska wrote: "All of us know that deceptive packaging and labeling techniques already constitute violations of existing law. The Federal Food, Drug, and Cosmetic Act prohibits misbranding and mislabeling. . . . The need for new laws to outlaw deception in packaging and labeling just does not exist. Such laws were provided long ago."

A long parade of hostile witnesses—individual businessmen, representatives of trade associations and chambers of commerce, and experts from the world of marketing and advertising—repeated this theme.

But expert advice had already been given the subcommittee on this question, and it showed clearly that existing law was wholly inadequate. The Library of Congress had given the subcommittee a 134-page report on all packaging and labeling laws and regulations under the jurisdiction of the Food and Drug Administration, the Department of Agriculture, the Department of Commerce, the Federal Trade Commission, the Bureau of Commercial Fisheries of the Department of the Interior, the Internal Revenue Service of the Department of the Treasury, the Bureau of Customs, the Coast Guard, the Interstate Commerce Commission, the Federal Aviation Agency, and the Post Office Department. After outlining existing packaging and labeling laws under each of these agencies, the report commented on the adequacy of the law with respect to each of the packaging abuses under scrutiny by the subcommittee.

Packaging to price, the insidious and widespread practice of reducing package contents while holding the package size constant, or redesigning it to make it look even larger, was perfectly legal. "No statutory provision or regulation dealing with this specific situation is found," said the Library of Congress report.

On the use of nonsense "jumbo" adjectives, said the report: "No reference is found in the above laws or regulations dealing specifically with limitations on quantity terminology."

On the much-abused cents-off deal, the report concluded that "this practice is not covered by the Food, Drug, and Cosmetic Act or regulations promulgated thereunder or by any other act listed above."

The question of servings is not mentioned in the report, and, since none of the laws or regulations outlined in the report touches on the question, it may be inferred that this practice is also not covered by existing law.

As for fractional-weight packages, which make it so difficult to compare prices, the report concluded: "No provision of the Food, Drug, and Cosmetic Act appears to be violated by this practice. The factor of standard packages is apparently involved. Some limitation of packages has been provided under other Federal laws. Examples are oleomargarine, wine, and distilled spirits." In addition to these, various state laws prescribe standard, rational net weights or liquid measures for packages of milk and cream, corn meal and grits, flour, oats, butter, bread, berries and small fruits, ice cream, beer, and animal feeds. The vast majority of packaged groceries, and all nonfood items such as soaps, detergents, waxes and polishes, and paper products, are completely unregulated.

Those who claimed that existing law was adequate usually cited Section 343 of the Federal Food, Drug, and Cosmetic Act, which reads, in part: "A food shall be deemed to be misbranded . . . If its labeling is false or misleading in any particular . . . If its container is so made, formed, or filled as to be misleading . . . [or] If any word, statement, or other information required by or under authority of this chapter to appear on the label or labeling is not prominently placed thereon with such conspicuousness (as compared with other words, statements, designs, or devices, in the labeling) and in such terms as to render it likely to be read and understood by the ordinary individual under customary conditions of purchase and use."

On the surface, this would appear to cover most deceptive packaging practices, but the statements in this section are so general and sweeping as to be very difficult to enforce. If the FDA believed a given package to be deceptive, it had to take the manufacturer into court and prove that, under Section 343, the labeling was "false" or "misleading," or that some statement on the label was not "conspicuous." These are concepts that are difficult to demonstrate legally, beyond reasonable doubt.

Usually, in a situation like this, the Congress gives the enforcing agency the power to issue regulations having the force of law which spell out the details of the broad legislative concept set forth in the statute. In the case of Section 343, Congress neglected to do this. As the Library of Congress report observed: "The FDA does not have authority to issue regulations having the force and effect of law regarding the provisions of this section. The regulations . . . are only advisory in nature." The FDA could and did issue regulations interpreting Section 343, but these were simply advisory to the manufacturers; that is, they indicated what the FDA interpretation of the law was. For the FDA to act successfully against a deceptive package, it still had to prove to the satisfaction of the court that the offending package was "so made, formed, or filled as to be misleading" or that its label lacked the proper degree of "conspicuousness." What was misleading or inconspicuous to the FDA might be something very different to a court.

This "case-by-case" method of policing packaging deception is very tedious and time-consuming. The FDA lacks the necessary manpower and other resources. Its primary obligation to the public is to prevent the sale of harmful foods and dangerous drugs, a task that could easily absorb all its energies and more. In 1960, for example, in nearly a thousand separate court actions, the agency removed from the market more than 7,700 tons of food for such reasons as insect infestation, mold, spoilage, contamination by fly eggs, maggots, rodent urine and "pellets," and high concentrations of insecticide residues. It stopped the sale of a vibrator-massager chair that was claimed by its manufacturer to successfully treat arthritis, cancer, heart disease, strokes, and kidney and liver conditions. It removed from the market an air purifier that was supposed to prevent poliomyelitis, tuberculosis, and strep throat. It seized an ultrasonic device that was advertised for treatment of sinus, thyroid, mastoid, and chest conditions. And it had its full quota of heart tonics, cancer creams, and elixirs for treating practically every human ailment, including arthritis, asthma, change of life, diabetes, epilepsy, cataract, hardening of the arteries, kidney stones, overweight, tapeworms, varicose veins, sciatica, headache, bursitis, vascular disease, ulcer, and high blood pressure.

Although the prior claim of human life and safety precluded any strong effort in the field of packaging deception, the FDA did make several attempts to prove packaging deception in the courts. In every case, it failed. The most celebrated of these cases, and one that typified the problem of proving deception under existing law, involved a box of chocolate-covered mints. The Delson Thin Mint case was dragging its way through the appeals courts even while the Senate hearings were under way.

In 1959, the FDA seized a shipment of chocolate-coated mints made by the Delson Candy Company of New York, charging that the package was "so made, formed, or filled as to be misleading." Thomas P. Wharton, president of Packaging Consultants, Inc., and a graduate civil engineer with long experience in the packaging field, described the package to the Senate subcommittee:

> I am convinced that the housewife who opens this package is shocked and bitter at the obvious steps which have been taken to reduce the quantity of mints in the package. In the inner package, the ends have been recessed a full half inch. Two hollow partitions have been provided, each of which occupies another half inch of space. This deception isn't even subtle. A full two inches of length has been faked within the package.
>
> Within the three compartments, there is enough additional space for six additional mints. The width and height of the box are sufficiently large to accommodate a mint one-quarter inch larger in diameter. It is significant to me that legitimate manufacturers put 60 per cent more of their mints in the same size box. . . . I understand that the company that now makes this deceptive package used to put a greater quantity of mints in this same box, but over a period of time has reduced the quantity without reducing the size of the container. . . . As a result of this type of competition, two other brands have resorted to recessed ends and hollow partitions. It is obvious that if such practices are allowed to continue, each company will try to out-do the other and deception will become standard practice.

As a packaging consultant, Mr. Wharton might have been expected to be a hostile witness, but the Delson package and others like it had brought him voluntarily to the Senate chamber to offer friendly testimony.

The FDA haled Delson into court as a test case. It had already lost three similar cases. Surely, if this one could not be won, the law needed strengthening.

While it was not necessary for the FDA to prove intent to deceive, only that the resulting package was deceptive, Delson defended its package by claiming that the recessed ends and hollow inner partitions were necessary to protect the mints from breakage. Even though independent engineering tests presented in court showed that the Delson box was not stronger than other boxes holding about twice as many mints, and even though the Delson box, which held thirty mints, was long enough to hold forty-one, the Federal District Court in Newark, New Jersey, ruled that there was insufficient evidence to support the charge.

The FDA appealed the decision, and, early in 1961, the Circuit Court of Appeals in Philadelphia sent the case back to the lower court for reconsideration. In June, 1961, the Newark District Court ruled again that the Delson mint package was not deceptive. In its decision, the court stated that the FDA statute on package deception was vague and indefinite. The FDA appealed once more to the Philadelphia court, but a year later its appeal was denied, thus closing the case. If ever a case demonstrated that a law was nonspecific and nonfunctional, this seemed to be it.

After the story of the Delson case had been put in the record of the hearings in 1961, S. Jerry Cohen commented, "Forty per cent of the [Delson] package was space; only 60 per cent was product. Yet the court found in that specific case this was not so filled as to be misleading. We feel if there were more specific standards as to what misleading means and what it doesn't mean, you wouldn't have the results of a court decision of this kind."

Mr. Cohen was, of course, questioning the adequacy of the law. Yet Minority Counsel Chumbris, representing Senator Dirksen's industry-oriented viewpoint in the hearings, chose to interpret Mr. Cohen's comment as a slur on the competence of the court. "Was the court decision erroneous? After all," he told Mr. Cohen, "they are the ones that are supposed to interpret the laws we pass."

This would not be the last time that Mr. Chumbris would choose to be irrelevant. Nor would it be the last time that Senator Hart would reveal the irrelevancy in a pithy retort: "I would say if they are right then we need to change the law." To say that present law was adequate, the senator went on, was analogous to saying the only law you need to have on the books was one preventing unreasonable behavior. To a citizen about to be beaten by a thug, it would be much more helpful to have a law specifically prohibiting assault and battery.

Despite the obvious implications of the Delson case, the opponents of the Hart bill continued to argue that existing law was adequate. At the opening of the 1963 hearings, Senator Dirksen stated: "There is no need for [the Hart bill]. I have found nothing in [this bill], under its mandatory provisions, which would give authority which does not already exist or is not already legal under existing law, and there is nothing in the testimony of the witnesses who appeared in 1961 and 1962 which would justify changing existing law dealing with the packaging industry."

The whole business was a serious waste of time, said Dirksen. "The Congress of the United States has before it many complex and serious matters affecting our domestic policies and our foreign relations policies to meet the crises that have kept the United States and other nations in the state of cold war since the end of World War II. I cannot see this Congress or any of its committees or subcommittees devoting valuable time to this bill when existing FDA and FTC laws have been sufficient in the past."

F. T. Dierson, general counsel for the Grocery Manufacturers of America, the giant food-industry trade association, denied that there was any problem of interpreting the meaning of existing law. "I have never found any difficulty in all my years of dealing with food manufacturers in explaining to them what a conspicuous label was, or in giving them a prompt judgment on submittal of a package as to whether it was conspicuous or not."

Mr. Cohen suggested to Mr. Dierson that some of the testimony and some of the package exhibits brought to the hearings indicated that there was no uniform understanding among food manufacturers of the meaning of the word "conspicuous." Mr. Dierson continued to deny this. "I think 'conspicuous' means easily legible," he maintained. He should have stopped there. In the next breath he cast some seeds of doubt himself. "There have been some situations," he went on, "where manufacturers have perhaps cut this fine, let us say, under the pressure of an advertising campaign, and perhaps under the advice of other than counsel."

In other words, some manufacturers, when the competition got too rough, or when advice from their lawyers was bad, lost sight of the fine sharpness of definition of the law. The editor of one packaging magazine put it a bit more baldly: "Lacking a clearly defined standard to which all could adhere," he wrote, "it is entirely possible that in the heat of competition some packagers have slipped into practices which in the most extreme interpretation of the word could be called 'deceptive.' No packager, except a stupid one, would be intentionally dishonest. But like all businessmen in our competitive free-enterprise system, a packager will go as far as the law allows in meeting competition."

There was no argument, then, that the packagers would push the law to the limit. Even their advocates admitted that. The only point of contention was, How far did the law allow?

The vice-president of Safeway Stores, J. Arnold Anderson, in a fascinating bit of testimony, all but admitted that some packages were under an ethical cloud but then, in the next breath, denied the need for new laws:

Senator Hart: Is there anything on your shelves that you would not approve, if produced by yourself? In other words, in this category is there anything on your shelves that would not pass muster out of your own processing plant?

Mr. Anderson: There might be. I know of no specific instances at the moment.

Senator Hart: In other words, do you apply the same standards to items that you get in to put on the shelves as you require of your own?

Mr. Anderson: No, I would not say that we do. We might be out of business in some items, but we do make suggestions. One of the biggest—

Senator Hart: Do you think there are items in great public demand which bear labels which you yourself would not put out?

Mr. Anderson: I believe that we would probably change them. Yes.

Senator Hart: So if you were to write the law, you would raise the level for those other labels?

Mr. Anderson: Well, as I stated, I do not see that a law is necessary.

Senator Hart: I stayed with you to the very last answer.

Senator Abraham A. Ribicoff, Democrat from Connecticut and former Secretary of Health, Education, and Welfare, brought into the hearing room three cans of baking powder and held them up for members of the subcommittee to see. The three cans were made by the same manufacturer, contained the same kind of baking powder, were exactly the same size, but had three different net weights: 16 ounces, 14.3 ounces, and 14 ounces. They were, he said, all on sale in the same store, at the same time, and at the same price. The net weights were printed vertically in an upper corner on two cans and horizontally at the bottom on the third. "I do not think it is normal," said Ribicoff, "to expect your wife or mine, the average housekeeper, to take the three cans out, the same size, the same label, the same markings, and start looking at all these cans to see if there is a difference. . . ."

Senator Hruska, the rock-ribbed conservative from Nebraska, attempted to make the point that the deception offered by the baking powder cans would be prohibited under existing law. Without challenging Hruska's premise on the grounds that the baking powder *had* been on sale in the supermarket, Senator Ribicoff replied, "You try to go into court, and you are sitting as a judge, and they bring in to you any one of those cans, and I do not think you could get a conviction from any judge or an order to cease and desist, or anything else, on the labels on the cans that I gave you. I think each one of those labels on those three cans of baking powder complies with the present law, and I cannot imagine a Secretary or a Commissioner of Food and Drug or the General Counsel's Office going into any court and trying to stop a practice like that under the authority that he now has."

The authority under existing law for moving against deceptive packaging was vested in the Food and Drug Administration (an agency of the Department of Health, Education, and Welfare) and the Federal Trade Commission (one of the independent Federal regulatory agencies set up by Congress to do its bidding). The respective laws were the Food, Drug, and Cosmetic Act and the Federal Trade Commission Act. The impotence of the FDA under the Food, Drug, and Cosmetic Act was amply demonstrated by fiascos such as the Delson Thin Mint case.

Under Section 5 of the Federal Trade Commission Act, the FTC is given the responsibility to prevent the use by businessmen of misleading or deceptive trade practices. Under Section 12 it has the duty to prevent false or misleading advertising. The FTC, like the FDA, has the power to issue advisory regulations under these sections, spelling out what it believes to be false or misleading or deceptive practices under the act. But, again, these regulations are advisory only, and any court action brought by the FTC under these sections would have to prove deception, not violation of the regulation.

Paul Rand Dixon, chairman of the FTC, was asked to appear before the subcommittee to verify this. The solid, gray Mr. Dixon, himself a former chief counsel and staff director of the Antitrust and Monopoly Subcommittee, said that the FTC has no authority to issue legislative regulations (that is, those having the force of law). Its regulations are advisory only.

"But," he was asked, "can't you bring these manufacturers in and tell them the Commission feels they are engaging in a deceptive trade practice within Section 5 or Section 12? And can't you then promulgate a regulation telling them the FTC views this particular practice as deceptive and telling them to change their methods?"

Mr. Dixon was skeptical. "Do you know how persuasive it would be?" he asked. "I think they would frown upon anyone telling them how to run their business. They would say, If I am wrong, you prove it."

This was the burden of the testimony of Mr. Dixon as to the Federal Trade Commission Act and of FDA Commissioner George P. Larrick as to the Food, Drug, and Cosmetic Act. Any regulations issued under these acts were purely advisory. Each time either agency sought to correct a malpractice by court action, it had to prove not a specific act of deception but rather the entire concept of deception. It was like re-inventing the wheel every time you needed a vehicle.

If existing law had been adequate during the fifteen years since the close of World War II, then the packaging industry, during all those years, must have been engaged in violation of the law on a staggering scale. Clearly, the law had not been adequate. Clearly, much more specific directions were needed by the packaging industry to help them decide which practices constituted deception. Until this could be done, the two regulatory agencies would be faced with prolonged and repeated court actions for every package that was deemed deceptive.

Both Chairman Dixon and Commissioner Larrick asked that the

subcommittee provide the needed legislation. Mr. Dixon stated that "enactment of a proper truth-in-packaging law, granting the Commission authority to issue regulations pertaining to packaging and labeling, would enable the Commission to protect the consumer from acts and practices which it may not be able, or it would be extremely difficult, to prevent under Section 5 of the Federal Trade Commission Act. Frequently the problem relating to proper packaging and labeling is . . . one of chaos and confusion rather than deception. Such a packaging law would dispel any doubt as to the ability of the Commission to prevent the continuation of such practices."

Mr. Larrick told the subcommittee: "The general terms of existing law regarding inconspicuousness have been impossible to enforce with uniformity. The improvement in this area to be achieved by [the Hart bill] is that regulations issued to implement the bill would in themselves have the force and effect of law. Thus, it would not be necessary to prove in each case that a particular label would be inconspicuous in the marketplace. . . . We believe that the truth-in-packaging bill represents a better approach in bringing about improvement in the packaging of consumer commodities than a program of enforcement on an individual commodity or a case-by-case basis under the present law."

The trouble with the existing law was that it had been written before the post-war methods of deception had been invented. Under the law, the FDA could ensure that manufacturers showed net weight somewhere on all food packages. Further, both the FDA and the FTC had been generally successful with cease-and-desist orders aimed at individual cases of slack fill. But beyond that they were all but helpless. Neither the blanket confusion caused by fractional weights and meaningless adjectives, nor the whole complex of deception known as packaging to price, nor the dishonesty implicit in the cents-off plague, could be touched by existing law. The Hart bill was aimed specifically at these practices.

The use of "large economy size" to describe a larger but more expensive size; the use of "giant" to describe a size smaller than a competitor's mere "large"; the use of "jumbo 14-ounce" to obscure the fact that the package had just been shrunk from a pound—such practices would be eliminated by Section 3(a)(3) of the Hart bill, which provided for regulations to "prohibit the addition to . . . statements of net quantity of contents of any qualifying words or phrases."

The use of fractional weights, wherever such use resulted in a confused or deceived consumer, would be eliminated by Section 3(c)(1), which provided that the FDA or the FTC could issue regulations, when necessary, to "establish reasonable weights or quantities, or fractions or multiples thereof, in which [a] commodity shall be distributed for retail sale." This section also was aimed at the elimination of packaging to price, as were Section 3(c)(2), which provided for regulations to "prevent the distribution of [a] commodity for retail sale in packages of sizes, shapes, or dimensional proportions" that might deceive the shopper "as to the net quantity of the contents thereof"; Section 3(a)(1), which required that the quantity be "stated upon the front panel of packages"; and Section 3(a)(2), which provided for regulations to "establish minimum standards with respect to the locations and prominence of statements of the net quantity of contents (including minimum standards as to the type size and face in which such statements shall be made)."

The abuse of cents-off promotion would be eliminated by Section 3(a)(5), which prohibited the *manufacturer* from placing on the package "any printed matter stating or representing by implication that such commodity is offered for retail sale at a price lower than the ordinary and customary retail sale price. . . ." Since the manufacturer had no control whatever over the retail price, it was perfectly reasonable that he be prohibited from making any promises about it on the package. This provision would eliminate those situations in which the promise of "cents off" appeared on the package, the manufacturer had reduced his price to the retailer accordingly, but the retailer had failed to pass along the reduction to the consumer. The bill would in no way restrict the retailer from cents-off promotions.

Other sections of the bill prohibited deceptive illustrations, provided for standard size designations (so that "giant" on one detergent box would mean the same as "giant" on a competitor's), and provided for standard "servings" designations (so that a "serving" of one canned fruit would mean the same as a "serving" of a competitor's).

In introducing his bill, Senator Hart stated that it was "not primarily directed at preventing fraud in the common law sense. It makes little difference to the economy and consumer whether price comparisons are made difficult or impossible because of fraud, deception, or only confusing practices. The seller's intent is not the important point—the practice and its effects are. Rather this legislation is aimed at bringing order out of the chaos of the modern marketplace as it pertains to consumable items—those most affected by the packaging revolution."

As he pointed out: "The need arises from the fact that, when marketing depends on prepackaging, the consumer cannot examine the product itself. He cannot look to the seller and get an assurance from him as to the product. Nor today can he readily compare products and their prices. Thus handicapped, the buyer has found it more difficult, if not impossible, to judge accurately the prices of competing products as a first step to making a rational choice between them."

Senator Hart insisted that his bill was designed not only to protect the consumer but also to protect the legitimate manufacturer from his less squeamish competitor. It was aimed at unfair competition which undermined the proper functioning of a free marketplace. For, when deceptive practices were allowed to succeed, they tended to spread by a Gresham's Law by which bad practices drove out the good, and the result was to debase the entire economy.

The Hart bill was an attempt to set up standards for packaging. Historically, manufacturing standards in any field are desired by the consumer and opposed by the producer. In this case, the consumer was the unorganized, largely apathetic housewife, represented by no powerful voice and representing no center of economic or political power. The voices being ranged in support of the Hart bill were the relatively weak ones of scattered, individual housewives, consumer organizations, professors of economics, women's clubs, and a handful of senators and congressmen.

Ranged against these voices was the largest and most powerful industry in the world—the food industry, whose $80-billion annual take was equal to that of the steel and automobile industries combined. The industry spoke through its articulate managers, trade associations, chambers of commerce, and well-heeled lobbyists. The industry all but controlled the channels of communication— the mass-circulation slick magazines and the television industry. It had as its ally the wordsmiths, thought managers, and motivationists of the advertising world.

With such powerful forces massed against it, the chances for passage of an effective packaging bill were slight. At one point in the battle, Senator Hart asked, "Can Federal legislation affecting consumers' economic interests be enacted?" The key word in the question was "economic." For the record showed that, even when the very health and life of the consumer was at stake, Congress had been exceedingly slow to act. Usually a catastrophe was necessary to blast legislation loose from reluctant legislators.

Take drugs, for example. Until 1938, the only Federal regulation of drugs and medicines was one requiring narcotics to be listed on the label. There were no restrictions whatever on advertising—manufacturers could make whatever claims they wished with impunity. There was no requirement that a drug be safe for human consumption. For years, bills were introduced in Congress to strengthen Federal drug laws, but they languished and died. Then, in 1937, more than a hundred people were killed by a new elixir of sulfanilamide. The next year, Congress passed the Food, Drug, and Cosmetic Act, which requires that a manufacturer— before marketing a new drug—prove to the government that it is safe when taken as directed. This eliminated from the market all the poisonous and habit-forming drugs that had sickened, killed, and addicted thousands of innocent consumers, but it left open to the manufacturer the entire field of false and fraudulent advertising, and it imposed no restriction on the sale of worthless drugs.

In 1961, Estes Kefauver introduced a bill to require manufacturers to demonstrate that a drug was truly effective before it could be marketed. This bill showed every symptom of dying quietly in Congress, but then the terrible international tragedies of thalidomide intervened. Newspaper headlines told of horribly deformed babies being born of mothers who had taken the drug. Public attention in the United States turned to the Kefauver drug bill, and Congress saw the light. After the vote in the Senate passing the bill, Paul Douglas of Illinois rose and asked, "Can we learn from this lesson, or can mankind educate itself only by disaster and tragedy?"

In the years following World War II, while the nation's schools fell deeper and deeper into decline, bill after bill was introduced in Congress to provide Federal aid to education. During the first six years alone, more than thirty bills were introduced, some 400 witnesses testified at hearings, and more than 4,000 pages of testimony piled up. But during these years of the most dire need, no help was given. Then, on October 4, 1957, the Russian Sputnik I vaulted into the sky, and the logjam in Congress was finally broken. The following year, the National Defense Education Act was passed. It is a clue to the system of values prevailing in Congress that the first Federal school aid bill was for "National Defense."

Although by 1965 more than a million United States citizens had been killed by automobiles, and over the previous decade hearing after hearing and bill after bill had explored the possibility of Federal action to reduce the carnage, it is doubtful that, even then, automobile safety legislation would have passed without the crusading fervor of author Ralph Nader and the widespread public attention attracted to his book, *Unsafe at Any Speed,* and to the scandalous behavior of General Motors Corporation in prying into his private life in an apparent attempt to discredit his testimony in Congress.

The national catastrophe attendant upon cigarette smoking is already upon us. This calamity has come, not by a single dramatic stroke, but rather through the slow and stealthy infusion of a million poisonous puffs. Therefore, Congress has found it impossible to act. After struggling mightily with the problem, the 89th Congress in 1966 brought forth a legislative sop requiring that cigarette packages bear the innocuous warning: "Caution: Cigarette Smoking May Be Hazardous to Your Health." Beyond that, the law actually *prohibits* any other health warning on the label, and it prohibits, until 1969, the imposition of any requirements that cigarette advertising include the health statement. Thus Congress made the world safe for cigarette advertising, at least until 1969, and thousands of our youth each year will be hooked on cigarettes and doomed to a premature death.

And so it goes. The question posed by Senator Douglas was not empty rhetoric. As Senator Joseph S. Clark of Pennsylvania wrote of Congress: "We bounce from one crisis to another, postponing solutions whenever possible. Finally, when things get bad enough, Congress legislates, often too little and too late."

If this is true of legislation in general, it is doubly true of legislation designed to benefit the consumer by restricting the freedom of action of a powerful business group. And if it is true of legislation bearing upon the health and safety of the consumer, it is doubly true of legislation bearing only upon his economic interest.

6

Packaging to Price

Of all the packaging abuses brought before the Hart subcommittee during its three years of hearings, the most economically damaging was the legerdemain known as "packaging to price," the practice of concealing a price rise behind a slight reduction in package contents. The woman who found her "quart" bottle of Lestoil reduced to 28 ounces, with no corresponding price reduction, was a victim of this dodge. Testimony offered at the hearings left no doubt that this practice was widespread. Opponents of the Hart bill, therefore, made no attempt to deny that the practice existed. They based their opposition on two arguments: (1) that there is nothing ethically wrong with the practice, and (2) that there is no intention to deceive on the part of the manufacturer, but that, on the contrary, he indulges in this practice in response to consumer demand.

The insidious nature of this practice and its power to force the well-meaning manufacturer to adopt packaging to price or lose the competitive struggle were illustrated by a number of witnesses. One of these was Harrison F. Dunning, former real estate broker, Fuller Brush salesman, and now executive vice-president of Scott Paper Company. Mr. Dunning had come to testify in opposition to the bill, but he nevertheless had unkind words to say about the difficulty of competing with those who nibbled away at the contents of their packages.

"During the war," he said, "when the Government established standards, as they had to for the war effort, they said that 125 feet is the unit for wax paper, everybody had to make it 125 feet. After the war, all of our competitors one after another dropped to 100 feet, because by so doing they had a price advantage, they thought, in terms of getting people to buy it. We stuck to 125 feet because we felt that this was the standard in the industry.

"We began to hurt in comparison with the 100 feet, so we tried a 75-foot length."

No nonsense here about response to consumer demand for a smaller size, or consumer surveys revealing a greater consumer convenience. Pure, raw competition.

It seems that wax paper is not the only kind of paper affected by this kind of competition. Staff Counsel Cohen asked Mr. Dunning: "I think you mention in your statement that the standard [for toilet tissue] is a thousand and 2,000. Yet we have seen many with 650 and 750 sheets. . . ."

Mr. Dunning: Now, where it gets to be tricky is where somebody cuts 50 sheets out and then makes it small. That is where I object to it.

Mr. Cohen: And this is the kind of discovery that the average person is not likely to make over even a long period of time, it not being the type of item you are likely to count after you get home?

Mr. Dunning: Yes. Of course, judging by our mail, it is amazing how many people will take the time to sit down and count the number of sheets in a roll of toilet paper.

The contagion of the disease was illustrated by the testimony of E. Lee Feller, general manager of Alliance Associates, an organization that specializes in the production and distribution of what are known as distributor-controlled brands of grocery products. The distributor-controlled brands appear on the supermarket shelves bearing such labels as Topco, IGA, Food Club, or Ann Page. They are identified with the supermarket chain itself, rather than with a nationally advertising manufacturer. Because they do not spend heavily for national advertising, they are usually less expensive than the nationally advertised, manufacturer-controlled brands.

Mr. Feller stated that this severe price competition from the distributor-controlled brands was one of the pressures that was forcing the manufacturer-controlled brands into the kind of "non-price competition" represented by packaging to price and other such practices.

"With supermarket merchandisers emphasizing their own controlled brands," said Mr. Feller, "giving them preferred shelf positions, preferred space allocations, preferred mass displays, we cannot deny that intensified merchandising efforts on the part of the national brand producers was called for and has necessitated constant product changes that they can promote in their advertising media, both television and point of sale, such as bigger packages and wider packages, that will catch the eye as the consumer moves down the shelf."

But then Mr. Feller told the subcommittee that the supermarket-controlled brands would have to fall in line if they hoped to survive. He cited the can of fruit cocktail as an example. Until recently, he said, fruit cocktail had been marketed in the No. 303 can, which holds about 16 ounces. Then the nationally advertised brands began to switch to the No. 300 can, which holds about 1 ounce less but is nearly indistinguishable from the No. 303 can without close examination. Naturally, the smaller can could be sold at a slightly lower price. But the hurried shopper, not realizing the difference in size, would grab the cheaper can. "What other alternative do we have," Mr. Feller asked the subcommittee, "other than to reduce the size of our own can?

"I should like to submit to this committee a sample of our present bottle of salad oil and to also submit to you a sample of that type of bottle that we are considering switching to. From this exhibit I think most observers would recognize that there might be somewhat less salad oil in the proposed new bottle, but I am sure most would not realize how much less. There is 32 ounces in the old bottle and 24 ounces in the proposed new bottle. Quite frankly, this change in bottle design is being prompted by the redesigning action of the large manufacturer-controlled salad oil brands. . . . For competitive reasons we are being forced to make this change."

Similar testimony was offered by representatives of consumer cooperatives, which are chains of supermarkets and other retail outlets owned and managed by and for the consumer. Donald Lefever, grocery buyer for Greenbelt Consumer Services, a consumer cooperative serving the Washington–Baltimore area, held up two bottles for all in the room to see. "These two bottles," he said, "represent a fruit flavored drink which has been selling on this market for approximately two years. The standard size had been one-half gallon, or 64 fluid ounces. This past spring we were informed by most of the packers that the new size would be 57 ounces, a reduction of 7 ounces. Some of these packers' representatives suggested that the consumer would not notice this change."

To thus impugn the motives of the food manufacturers was to arouse the wrath of Senator Dirksen's minority counsel, Peter Chumbris. Flushing to the roots of his widow's peak, Mr. Chumbris shot back at Mr. Lefever: "Since the industry . . . felt that 57 ounces was the one that was selling, what is wrong with that? Why is 64 ounces anything that should seem to be more sacred than a 57-ounce jar if the price is consistent, taking into consideration whatever increased cost there may be in the production of the article? What is so sacred about 64 ounces and this particular jar?"

There was, of course, nothing "sacred" about 64 ounces. This was one of those questions that avoid the heart of the matter and are impossible to answer in any rational manner. Mr. Lefever replied simply that "The industry had made a record of having 64 ounces for several years prior to this time. Suggestions by some of the representatives of the industry were that the consumer would not note the change, and I think that clearly establishes—"

This second reference to improper suggestions by the industry was apparently too much for Mr. Chumbris, who, abandoning logic, interrupted: "You do not know that for a fact. You do not know as a definite fact, that every manufacturer in the United States who reduces the contents of his product feels that he, the consumer, will not recognize the difference? Would you make that flat statement? After all, this is a congressional committee that wants to get—"

"Just a minute, Mr. Chumbris," Senator Hart broke in. "He did not make that statement. We all heard what he said."

Whereupon Mr. Chumbris returned to his theme of the sanctity of size. "The point I am making is, what is so sacred about a 64-ounce jar and how did they arrive at the 64 ounces in the first place?"

At which Mr. Lefever found it necessary to inform Mr. Chumbris that 64 ounces is "a half-gallon, which, I think, that you would recognize is a standard in our measurement system."

Another witness was even less kind in his appraisal of the manufacturer's motives. Colston E. Warne, professor of economics at Amherst College and president of Consumers Union, minced no words. "Competition in many fields," he said, "is competition in deception rather than competition in price. The deviations in size are not deviations for the purpose of serving the consumer. Some companies are trying to sneak by on that supermarket shelf with a smaller quantity of goods at an effective higher price per ounce."

Again, Mr. Chumbris rose to the defense of the maligned manufacturer. "But you don't bear in mind the manufacturer's point of view. He has a choice of either raising the price or lowering the content. For his specific reasons, which he has a God-given right to do under the American way of life and the competitive system, he has a choice of doing one or the other. You keep saying it is deception and you don't give him any credit at all for any honesty in his judgment, as to why he prefers to lower content rather than raise the price. I think we ought to get that point pretty well straight at this point. You don't give him any credit whatsoever."

Again and again, Mr. Chumbris and other defenders of the practice of packaging to price came back to the morality of the thing. Regardless of his intent, they seemed to say, the manufacturer, as a free-born American, has a "natural" right to manipulate the size of the package to suit his purposes, without regard to its effect on the consumer, the marketplace, the economy, or the national welfare. Here is a manufacturer, they said, faced with an increase in his manufacturing costs. He has two alternatives: he can raise the price of his package or he can reduce its contents. He should have the right to make that decision. "Is there anything wrong with that?" Mr. Chumbris asked. "This freedom to adjust the price in package sizes is basic and must be preserved under our free enterprise system of business. As stated, there is nothing wrong with it, legally or otherwise."

This is complete nonsense. There is no such basic right either stated or implied in the United States Constitution or in Western philosophy. Had there been such a basic right, then the packagers of milk, butter, flour, sugar, and whiskey, to name a few, were suffering an infringement of their rights, since the law requires these commodities to be packaged in standardized amounts. The test of whether or not an economic act is wrong is in its effect on the marketplace. If it can be shown that packaging to price is harmful to the consumer and to the proper functioning of the free, competitive economy, then it is wrong.

And the overwhelming weight of the evidence was that the practice is harmful. Witness after witness stated that too often the consumer was unaware of what had happened to the contents and the price and was thereby deceived, whether or not the manufacturer had intended to deceive. And too often it appeared that the manufacturer *had* intended to deceive. The outspoken Professor Warne told of the hundreds of letters received by Consumers Union: "The point that runs through all these letters . . . is that where a manufacturer sneaks in on a back corner in exceedingly fine print the statement of a reduced amount and uses motivational research techniques to make the package look far larger than it is, and, somehow or other, a couple of ounces disappear in the procedure, this constitutes a straight deceit."

The practice can be condemned simply on the grounds that the consumer should be permitted to know what is going on so that he can have a better chance of making a rational choice in his food shopping. He is in the act of spending a large share of his pay check. He deserves to have every break, every piece of pertinent information, in making his selection. Any impediment to the free flow of this marketing information works to his personal detriment and also to the detriment of the honest manufacturer by rewarding the shady one for his deceit.

The obstruction to the free flow of information has wider implications than simply deception of the housewife, as was brought out by another professor of economics: "I think that raising prices is a fairer method of proceeding in a competitive situation than reducing quantity, because people know better where they are. . . . Inflation in our economy is a very serious question, and we ought to be able to handle it in the open . . . where its causes can be more effectively diagnosed, and, hopefully, cures developed." Housewives who testified agreed. They would prefer, they said, to see the price of the package go up, with the contents the same, so they would know how much more they were paying for it.

One industry witness, R. Allan Hickman, vice-chairman of the All-Industry Packaging Advisory Committee, had the temerity to suggest that "Varying the weight is a legitimate and proper marketing method which benefits the consumer." He did not expand on how this practice was supposed to benefit the consumer, but it was a peculiar position to take in the face of letter after letter from consumers who stated they felt insulted and deceived because it appeared that the manufacturer thought they would not understand that a drop in quantity at the same price was a price increase.

Mr. Hickman continued that variable weights are neither maliciously inspired nor intended to deceive; they merely acknowledge a basic fact of life. If costs go up, something has to give. The quantity can be reduced, or the quality can be lowered to provide the same quantity for the same price. "Public reluctance to pay more may drastically reduce the sales of the manufacturer who raises his prices," he concluded, perpetuating the fiction that a quantity reduction is not a price increase. What he meant, of course, was that a quantity reduction is, in the words of the marketeers, "more acceptable" to the consumer; that is to say, less noticeable and therefore more readily swallowed.

Finally, said Mr. Hickman, to deprive the manufacturer of the right to use this valuable marketing tool would be to deprive the consumer of something very precious to him. "Legally dictated standardization of either size, weight, or quantity will result in depriving the shopper of a choice of quantity and hence of price which may be very important to the consumer." Presumably, the housewife cherishes the right to discover, if she can, whether the new package of 14½ ounces at 73 cents is more or less expensive than the old one at 16 ounces for 79 cents.

The question of the manufacturer's intent—whether he intends to deceive the consumer or whether he chooses the packaging-to-price method of raising prices for some other reason—was, as Senator Hart pointed out more than once, not at issue. The question was, What is the effect of this practice on the consumer and how does it affect the functioning of the marketplace? But, since the opponents of the bill chose, for the most part, to ignore the main question of effect and to base most of their defense on the premise of innocent motives on the part of the manufacturer, it is enlightening to explore the question of motive.

We have already heard a number of witnesses—the vice-president of Scott Paper Company, the general manager of a company producing distributor-controlled grocery products, a grocery buyer for a cooperative grocery chain, and a professor of economics—state that the motive for reducing package contents is purely and simply to gain a competitive advantage. Further, three of the four witnesses implied, and one stated very explicitly, that the move is made with the express intent to deceive the consumer. Finally, it is difficult to understand how the manufacturer can achieve a competitive advantage unless the consumer *is* deceived, since, in almost all cases of quantity reduction, the price is, in effect, boosted.

One witness, a professor of political economy at Columbia University, told the subcommittee that an increase in manufacturing costs is not the only stimulant to quantity reduction. "Temptations to reduce quantity while maintaining package size need not necessarily arise from the necessity of meeting an increase in costs of production or distribution," he testified. "It may be a device to widen margins, either to increase profits, to provide for a larger advertising budget, or to compensate for a failure to achieve competitive standards of efficiency in some phase of the firm's operations."

In other words, this "marketing tool" is destructive to the maintenance of a free, competitive market, since it enables the less efficient producer to compensate for his inefficiency rather than be driven out of the market by his more efficient competitor, in accordance with the theory of free competition.

Robert L. Andrews, packaging manager for Topco Associates, a producer of distributor-controlled grocery products, opposed legislation to control packaging to price. "Requiring that various sizes be kept in common multiples, or in weights consistent with arbitrary decisions, could again hamper the merchandising programs of the suppliers or their retailers," he said. Then he went on to describe the kind of merchandising program that would be hampered. "Supplier A may wish to introduce their new product X into a very competitive market of 32-ounce products. Because of special packaging, such as a reusable container, plus the high costs of advertising and promotion required to establish a new product in the market, company A may have to select a 28-ounce contents package to provide the moneys required to put their product over and yet remain competitively priced. To require a 32-ounce contents could prohibit this new (and possibly better) product entry into the market."

The picture painted of our free, competitive market by Mr. Andrews is frightening. Apparently it is no longer possible for a new (and possibly better) product to make its way in the marketplace without resorting to devious packaging. The shoppers are too stupid, or too apathetic, to perceive the improved quality or enhanced "convenience" and be willing to pay for it. Instead, they have to be tricked into paying for it. On the other hand, Mr. Andrews was saying, this valuable "marketing tool" is needed by the manufacturer to fool the unwary shopper into paying the high cost of advertising necessary to establish a new product in a highly competitive market. Either way, the costs come out of the housewife's purse.

Under questioning by Mr. Cohen, some of the verbiage in Mr. Andrews's testimony about "merchandising programs," "special packaging," and "better product" was stripped away. Slowly, patiently, the quiet-spoken young lawyer picked away at the fog of jargon to reveal the kernel of truth. Responding to this treatment, Mr. Andrews gradually discarded polysyllabic generalities and began to speak in basic English.

First, Mr. Cohen persuaded him to agree that most of the reductions in package content are initiated by the manufacturers of national brand products. Then he asked whether Mr. Andrews would agree that one of the reasons for this was to give the national brand products a competitive edge over the distributor-controlled brands.

"I wish I knew what many of the national brand people were doing," Mr. Andrews replied, "because it would be of great help to me in my job. I do not know all of the reasons why they do it. I would presume that would be one of them. . . . It could be one of the reasons, yes."

Then Mr. Cohen suggested to Mr. Andrews that the only recourse for the manufacturer of the distributor-controlled brands would be to respond in kind by nibbling away at the contents of his packages "so these things chase each other by the tail around the circle to keep up?"

"That is correct," agreed Mr. Andrews. "As soon as they . . . get so small, somebody brings out a 2-pound family size and the circle starts all over again."

Mr. Andrews had thus testified to the chain reaction whereby packaging to price sweeps through the supermarket. The next question was, What causes the brand-name manufacturer to set off the chain reaction in the first place? "Would you say," Mr. Andrews was asked, "that in most of those cases, where there is a change in package size, it is because there has been a new discovery, an improvement in the product, and, therefore, they find that now they can have a smaller quantity do the same job, and they cut down on the package, or is it in order to cover up for an increase in price, or what?"

"I feel," Mr. Andrews replied, "that reductions in weights are to compensate for an increase in raw product or finished price."

There it was. No more nonsense about consumer convenience or breaking a better product into the market. Then Mr. Cohen proceeded to pin down one more explanation that had been offered by the champions of this marketing tool: "Do you know of any instances," he asked, "where, let's say, the package sizes decreased because the producer had conducted some research and found out that so much of the contents earlier were wasted, so now he is going to have a smaller quantity so nothing will be wasted?"

Mr. Andrews said he did not know of any.

With such testimony in mind, it is instructive to browse among the statements of the hostile witnesses to collect some of their thoughts about the motives behind the exercise of this marketing tool.

Waste, for example. Some manufacturers maintained that the smaller package had been adopted because they had found that the consumer opened the larger package, used some of it, then wasted the leftovers. Mr. Andrews, packaging manager for a firm serving twenty-five supermarket chains and wholesale grocery companies, with ten years' experience in the business, had told the subcommittee that he had never heard of any reduction in packaging contents being made for that reason. Mr. Chumbris asked: "But the reduction of content may not be to take care of price at all. It may be because the manufacturer, who may have found in their surveys that a 303 can may better serve the public than a No. 2 can, because there is no wastage or—"

"That is possible," said Mr. Andrews.

"Is that right?" Mr. Chumbris persisted.

"That is possible," repeated Mr. Andrews.

Anything, of course, is possible.

The executive vice-president of the National Association of Food Chains, C. G. Adamy, told the committee that a primary reason for packaging to price was that "a good many consumers purchased by price and not by quantity." This statement, taken out of context, is a little difficult to interpret. One would think that most rational customers purchase by both price *and* quantity— how many ounces for how many cents. Then Mr. Adamy gave the nickel candy bar as an example. Consumers, he said, prefer a candy bar for a nickel.

Possibly. But perhaps this conclusion was reached by the following route: Candy bar makers A and B both make a 2-ounce bar for a nickel. The price of chocolate and sugar go up. Candy maker A raises the price of his bar to 6 cents. Candy maker B keeps the nickel price but reduces the weight of his bar to 1⅝ ounces. The consumer indicates a "preference" for the nickel bar by switching his allegiance from bar A to bar B. But what would his preference have been if he had realized that bar B, the nickel bar, was actually more expensive?

In the case of the candy bar, admittedly, two points must be granted. Some consumers, wishing not to be bothered with the handling of pennies in the transaction, would prefer to pay the nickel for the more expensive bar as a "convenience." Secondly, many candy bars are dispensed by machine, and here the nickel is plainly the more efficient price to pay. But it must finally be stated that the candy bar is not the typical grocery item, and in any case the facts of the matter should be clearly available to the consumer so that he can make his choice in a rational manner.

Edmund W. J. Faison, president of an organization known as Visual Research, Inc., a firm that applies the principles of psychology and consumer motivation to the design of packages, introduced a scholarly note into the hearings. "Take liquid salad dressings," he began. "A recent change has taken place in the industry in that the size has been reduced. And now, again, it cannot be denied that this package holds less. . . . But that is not the reason for the change. First, the salad dressing bottle is one that is often brought to the table and the appearance of the bottle itself is important. Second, there has been quite an increase lately in the concern for calories. Housewives much prefer a slimmer shaped bottle than the bulkier looking bottle, which is less attractive on the table."

His long face expressionless behind dark-rimmed glasses, Senator Hart asked Dr. Faison what relationship there was between the shape of the bottle and the concern for calories.

"Well," replied Dr. Faison, "it is interesting, because in the same way as with your soft drink bottles, housewives that are given to the slim line look prefer the bottles to be the same thing."

Senator Hart was just being hard to get. No doubt Dr. Faison had some experimental data to show that calorie-conscious housewives, subconsciously associating the slimmer bottle with a lighter, less fattening oil, reached for the slimmer bottle on the supermarket shelf. It was just a stroke of good luck that the oil manufacturers were thereby able to snitch a few ounces from the slimmed-down bottle.

The consumer-motivation authority plugged hard at the angle of consumer preference. Study after study had been made, said Dr. Faison, on many different packages, and most of them showed conclusively that the consumer "preferred" the smaller package. And these were not just academic laboratory studies. "I mean controlled experiments," he stated, "in which we have gone into supermarkets with alternate designs after manufacturers have come to us and asked us, 'What do consumers want? Do they want a package that has a little less in it, or do they want to pay a little more?' "

If those were truly the questions asked by the manufacturers, Dr. Faison and his Visual Research organization used a curiously ineffective method of getting the answer. Did they devise a questionnaire and an interviewing technique with which they could elicit the answer from the housewife? They did not. They prepared two packages, one that "has a little more quantity but sells for a little more, and the other version sells for a little less and there is a little less quantity." They put them in two different supermarkets and sat back to see which ones sold best against the existing competition. Could there be any question which package the consumers "preferred"? The more expensive or the less expensive package? Dr. Faison and Visual Research were not answering the question, What do consumers want? They were answering the question, What will the consumers buy? And, one suspects, this was the question the manufacturers asked.

In any event, Dr. Faison's answer was that "they would prefer not to spend more. They would rather have a little less. But this is not a matter of deceit. This is a matter of bringing the consumer what she wants, based on actual sales and comparative sales tests. Our studies have shown time and again that consumers would prefer to have quantity decreased rather than prices raised."

The studies by Dr. Faison and Visual Research showed no such thing. They showed, instead, that most consumers did not realize what the true price comparison was between the smaller package and its competitors.

Senator Hart pointed up the absurdity of Dr. Faison's conclusions by asking: "What result would you get if this kind of test was run? Rather than having your people observe the larger sized, higher priced, old style bottle in one store, and, in some other store, the new bottle of the smaller size and lower price, suppose you ran a test that put both of these on parallel shelves and identified clearly what they are—whatever the old one was, 32 ounces at 50 cents, and the new one at its side was 28 ounces at 46 cents, what would happen then?"

Dr. Faison professed to be ignorant of what would happen then. But when Senator Hart suggested to him that such a test might be a very good way to find out what the consumer really wants, the motivational researcher agreed that "this may be a very good idea." Then, with astonishing artlessness, he asked the senator: "Do you feel that [the net weight] would have to be on the front of the panel or package?"

Senator Hart hesitated, then with a slight edge of annoyance in his usually courteous tone, he answered: "I am indifferent as long as we do not have to be a stunt man to find it. Just as long as it is there clearly and simply. We have heard a lot of static about that."

Another motivational researcher who testified was Louis Cheskin, director of a firm called Marketing Research and Color Research Institute and author of a book titled *Why People Buy*. At the end of his prepared testimony, which was filled with wisdom about the "psychological communication" of the package and its role as the "visual manifestation" of the product, Senator Hart asked: "Well, now, you heard me this morning express my view about the fellow who has been marketing in a package this size, 32 ounces or 80 sheets. Then he decides that he is going to market 28 ounces or 60 sheets, and the package changes this way [moving his hands together to indicate shrinkage]. What is the special reason for that?"

"It could be," replied Mr. Cheskin thoughtfully, "that he just had those packages—"

"No," the senator broke in impatiently, "I am talking about the fellow who reduces his quantity and puts it into a package that, on the shelf, appears larger than the package that previously held his larger volume. You talk about the psychological reasons behind package changes. What is the psychology behind that fellow? What is it?"

"Of course, there could be a motivation to give the impression of greater size," Mr. Cheskin admitted. "There could be such motivation."

Still dissatisfied, the senator dug at the equivocation: "What are the motivations?"

But Mr. Cheskin slipped away. "Well, motivations for getting those particular cartons. It often happens. I have seen that happen personally, when you could get those cartons, even though they are bigger, cheaper than smaller sizes because these were a stock run and smaller cartons would require a special run. Such things do exist."

As one earlier witness had said, "That is possible."

One of the most educational reasons given for the use of the packaging-to-price tool was offered by Thursten Clarke, editor of *Food & Drug Packaging*. "Considerable anger has been aroused," he stated, "by a propensity on the part of some manufacturers to reduce quantity while maintaining price. This is a perfectly legitimate method of easing the burden of inflation which constantly plagues our economy." Fascinating. How a price increase, disguised as a packaging change, could "ease the burden of inflation" is a subject for deep contemplation. Perhaps the inflation Mr. Clarke had in mind was the inflation of package sizes.

E. Lee Feller, the producer of so-called distributor-controlled grocery brands whose earlier testimony had indicated that much of the packaging-to-price turmoil was the result of a competitive struggle between the nationally advertised brands and the less expensive distributor-controlled brands, pointed out that the package from which a few ounces has been removed got the better break from the retailer because he could usually make a bigger profit from it.

"The extra ounce taken out of a newly designed package," he

said, "might make it possible for the retailer to buy a case of the item at a slightly lower price than previously, and if the same retail price is maintained his gross margin can be increased to enable him to pay higher wages and meet other rising expenses. . . . The simple facts are that a slight decrease in weight of an item is a more palatable increase in consumer cost than would be a retail price increase in items that have a long established price pattern."

For "more palatable" read "more easily put over on the consumer."

This type of deceptive marketing practice is especially effective with the younger shopper, who could be presumed to be less knowledgeable about the traps that are laid for her along the aisles of the supermarket. The president of a macaroni company was explicit on this point: "In order to keep reasonable price differences between high quality and lower quality products, it is sometimes necessary to reduce the size of the package—for example from 8 ounces to 7 ounces . . . and with your new consumers coming each year this is very important, not so much with the older ones but with the new girls that come and buy in the grocery store each for the first time. . . . By following such a policy, we have built a successful business."

No question about it: it's better to get 'em young. Some of those older ones are pretty wily.

As the trade association for the $80-billion food industry, the richest and most powerful industry in the world, Grocery Manufacturers of America brought enormous muscle to bear against packaging legislation. The president of GMA, Paul S. Willis, was one of the more voluble witnesses to appear before the committee. The picture of well-fed success, his round, almost cherubic face topped by a balding forehead, Mr. Willis spent many hours at the witness table in faithful, dogged, but uninspired antagonism toward the Hart bill. He had spent all his business life in the food industry, since 1933 as president of GMA, and his hostility to packaging legislation was unalloyed, if his testimony was sometimes maladroit.

In his prepared statement, Mr. Willis touched on the reason for reduction in package sizes. "Why do manufacturers sometimes discontinue certain package sizes and offer different ones? This could especially happen in the case of new products where it takes a while for consumer buying experience to establish the preferred package sizes. Sometimes later experience indicates that a package of a different size is preferable to the original one. This was true in frozen vegetables. Originally, they were packaged in 12-ounce sizes, and when it was found out later that a 10-ounce size was preferred by consumers, manufacturers supplied it."

Staff Counsel Cohen was curious to know how this consumer "preference" had been discovered by the frozen food manufacturers. "You say as to frozen vegetables," he asked, "originally they were packaged in 12-ounce sizes and it was found out later that a 10-ounce package was preferred by consumers and manufacturers supplied it?"

Mr. Willis: Yes.

Mr. Cohen: There have been some people in the frozen food industry who have suggested to us that the reason for this change was not because the consumer preferred the 10-ounce size, rather the reason was because one of the national brand manufacturers cut his size to 10 ounces for competitive reasons; not because the consumer wanted it, but to give himself a competitive advantage, and, as a result, the other manufacturers followed him.

Mr. Willis: Well, we hear a lot of statements based on another man's statement, and a lot of times such statements are made because the person has an ax to grind. . . . I hear many statements like you just made, and when you examine them, in many instances you find that the person has a personal ax to grind or has some prejudiced reason. . . .

Mr. Cohen: Let us take an example here. In this frozen food field, in the supermarket today, we see a lot of 9-ounce packages in certain lines coming out and replacing their old 10-ounce packages. Do you mean to say that there are surveys which show that a consumer would rather have 9 ounces of frozen vegetables than 10?

Mr. Willis: I did not say that.

Mr. Cohen: That type of change would not be based on consumer preference?

Mr. Willis: I said, when manufacturers originally came out with frozen foods, they had no basis to go by as to what was the preferred size. After a while, experience showed that 10 ounces was preferable so they changed to 10. Why they went to nine, I do not know.

Mr. Cohen: Do you have some surveys that indicate that consumers preferred 9 ounces rather than 10 ounces?

Mr. Willis: There must be, because I don't believe they would make such a change without that.

Mr. Cohen: If you could locate such a survey, we would appreciate it.

Mr. Willis: I would not know who might have such information. . . .

Mr. Cohen: We have heard a lot about this rising cost of business being the reason that sizes are often reduced. There were, I think, one or two witnesses yesterday who suggested that probably one of the primary reasons for cutting sizes was to put the national brand distributor in a better competitive position with the private labeler, who usually has to follow suit in this area. Would you comment on that?

Mr. Willis: There you get back to the people who have a personal ax to grind.

Mr. Cohen: What is your opinion? Do you think there is any validity to this?

Mr. Willis: My opinion is that responsible manufacturers do not make changes unless they are sure that it meets the preferences and acceptances of the public. That is their only customer, the public.

Mr. Cohen: Then actually, there are a number of reasons that might contribute to the lowering of contents in approximately the same sized bottle, rather than just the increase of the cost of manufacturing the product?

Mr. Willis: There might be. Maybe consumer usage has changed. But there had better be a reason which satisfies the consumer.

Mr. Cohen: I find it hard to understand, particularly in the liquid detergent area, why a consumer would prefer 15 ounces instead of a pint, which has happened recently in two of these detergents.

Mr. Willis: I would not know.

Senator Hart, who had sat through day after day of this kind of testimony with patience and forbearance, and whose characterization of some of the testimony as "static" was a rare show of petulance, offered a summation at one point with some feeling: "I must say that, as I listen day after day to this discussion about psychiatrists and motivational experts who decide that the consumer would not buy if, for any number of reasons, you had an increased price, and the wise thing, therefore, is to reduce the content, I get the feeling that a lot of this hocus-pocus obscures the fact that in the heart of a great many of these people, who decide they are going to trim back on their quantity instead of laying it on the line and increasing the price, is the hope that the consumer will not know what has happened."

The senator had abandoned his customary tone of quiet courtesy. "In my book," he went on, "or to many of us who have been talking about it, it is really a motivation that goes this way: Everybody is used to their 32-ounce box. Call in the package fellow and get him to make a box that looks even bigger. Be sure to put on the label some place that we have cut it back to 28, but chances are pretty good that Joe Consumer will not know what has happened.

". . . The reason we trim that quantity instead of jacking up the price is because we have a sneaky suspicion that a good many buyers will not know why it is that the box does not feed as many people as it did last week.

"That is a harsh thing to say, but I believe it."

7

The Shattered Ounce

One of the objections to fractional net weights is that it enables the manufacturer to nibble away at the contents of his packages unbeknownst to the housewife. Another is that the housewife finds it very difficult to calculate the price per ounce.

If all crackers, for example, were packaged in 1-pound or ½-pound boxes, it would be relatively simple for the shopper to decide which crackers are least expensive. This is not to say, of course, that most housewives would make their buying decision on the basis of price alone, but price would certainly be at least one of the factors in her buying decision, and it seems only reasonable to suppose that the price would be made readily available to her by the manufacturer.

Not so. One housewife told the Hart subcommittee about a cracker-buying experience. "Right next to the detergents are five packages of crackers. Crackers are an item that mothers buy a lot of. Children like to eat crackers all day long, it seems. They all are the same size." (We must assume that the witness was referring here to the cracker boxes, not the children.)

"Instead of being able to decide just by comparing prices, since I am a shopper who is aware that you cannot always tell by the outside size of the package, I look at the labels to find out the weight. I find out here that these crackers weigh—one 8 ounces, one 8½ ounces, one 9½ ounces, one 9¾ ounces, and one 10 ounces.

"It seems that the simple concept of a pound or a half-pound has just been thrown out the window. You might think we had never heard such simple weights."

The housewife doubted the manufacturer's motives: "Now it does not seem to me that this kind of packaging comes as a result of consulting consumers' wishes. This consumer would much prefer packages in even multiples of ounces or pounds or pints. It would save me untold woman-hours and make me feel that I was doing a much more competent job in making my purchases. . . . Is somebody trying to fool somebody by making you feel that because you have the same size package, a difference of 30 per cent in a weight should be ignored? I do not know. I cannot believe that they are trying to be honest."

There would seem to be little justification for such a profusion of weights. In some products, it is true, the practice can be rationalized. Canned soups, for example. For efficient and economical packing, shipping, and storing, it seems reasonable to standardize on a single size of can for all kinds of soup. But the densities—that is, the weights per unit volume—of different kinds of soup are not identical. Vegetable soup may be more dense than chicken noodle. So, if you fill two similar cans with the same volume of each soup, the can of vegetable soup will weigh slightly more.

Manufacturers of other products—detergents and dry breakfast cereals, for example—gave the same argument in defense of fractional-weight packages. For more efficient production, they said, different products having different densities were packaged in cartons of the same size. In this way, one line of very expensive packaging machinery, set up to handle a carton of a given size, could be used to package several different products.

Whatever merit there might have been to their argument was weakened by several observations made during the hearings. First, the allowable fill tolerances for dry bulk material in a cardboard carton were much greater than for a liquid soup in a can. A survey by Consumers Cooperative of Berkeley, California, made in the spring of 1965, revealed that the net weight in a box of Wheat Chex had dropped from 1 pound 2 ounces to 14½ ounces, Corn

Chex from 9 to 8 ounces, and Sunshine Shredded Wheat from 12 to 11 ounces, *all without any change in carton size.*

Second, the detergent men insisted that the different formulas in detergents gave them different densities, thus contributing to the odd-weight packaging problem. A hint as to the source of this problem was carried in an advertisement in *Chemical Week* for a detergent ingredient manufactured by Hooker Chemical Corporation. The headline read: "How spray-dried phosphates give your detergents 30% more bulk at the same cost . . . and the same weight." Hooker was inviting detergent manufacturers to inflate their product with air to increase profits. "The secret's in the hollow centers," the ad read. "When sodium phosphates are spray-dried, each granule has an air bubble in its middle. This makes them 70% bulkier than conventional phosphates.

"You can plainly see what this bulky phosphate will do when you put it in your detergent. Its 70% greater mass adds 20% to 30% to your package size (depending on the amount used)—and *nothing* to your cost."

It had been well known that the primary ingredient of many breakfast cereals was air, but it was of interest to learn that the detergent manufacturers could avail themselves of the same flexibility.

Finally, many witnesses before the subcommittee maintained that the profusion of sizes was the result not so much of consumer need as of the manufacturer's need to increase the amount of shelf space devoted to his products in the supermarket.

F. J. Schlink, technical director of Consumers' Research, told the subcommittee: "There would seem to be no good reason why products such as bread and milk can be and are sold in even or simple multiples of pints and pounds, whereas . . . all sorts of food products are sold in an almost infinite variety of package sizes, not only with odd ounces, but often with fractions of an ounce."

For example, Mr. Schlink said, "Popular silver polishes are offered in all of the following sizes: 7, 7½, 8, 12, 14, and 16 ounces. Two simply related sizes, 8 and 16 ounces, should suffice to cover this range of values. There can be no good reason for deviation in the weight of packages of approximately the same size, from a standard or normal value, except the convenience of the manufacturer of the product and his interest in making it impossible for consumers to make comparisons of price easily and quickly and without the aid of a computing device, such as the engineer's slide rule. It is not easy to decide upon a system of standard weight and volume values for the contents of bottled and packaged items, because of variations in density, consistency, and other factors; but there is reason to believe that a workable system could be constructed by experts on size standardization without difficulty. Such a system would do no serious injustice to any manufacturer but would be of very great value to consumers."

Besides milk and bread, a few other items had escaped the fractional weight disease. Sugar, flour, and ground coffee were still packaged in even pounds. Fresh fruits and vegetables were still priced and sold by the pound. But most of the acreage in the supermarket shelves was filled with bottles, boxes, cans, jars, and cartons. The price of their contents was anybody's guess. Democratic Congresswoman Leonor K. Sullivan of Missouri wrote that "the careful shopper absolutely needs a slide rule and the knowledge of how to use it in order to divide fractions of ounces into so-many-for-so-much prices if she is to estimate even roughly whether the large economy size is a better value than the smaller size. Often the answer is that it is not a better value—that the large size costs disproportionately more. And this answer always comes as a shock, as if the manufacturers and retailers—after spending years educating the consumer to believe the larger size is always more economical—are now cashing in on that induced belief by deliberately turning it against the consumer and cheating the purchaser. For that is exactly what the packaging rat race seems to represent."

If the need for a slide rule seemed an exaggeration of the problem, many housewives seemed to feel otherwise. They began to appear in the supermarkets, pushing their carts with one hand and clutching their slide rules in the other. Enterprising manufacturers were marketing slide rules especially for grocery shopping, under such names as "E-Z Bargain Finder," "The Housewife's

Friend," "The Thrifty Shopper," and "CTC Shopping Computer."
The December, 1961, issue of *Science and Mechanics* contained
directions for making a shopper's slide rule. Unfettered enterprise
had turned the marketplace into a jungle, and the housewives who
valued their economic lives were bearing arms in their defense.

Some opponents of truth in packaging maintained that the
housewife did not really care to know the truth, that loyalty to
brand name was paramount in a shopping decision. In her turn
at the witness table, Mrs. Sarah Newman, who was testifying as a
housewife and also as a member of the board of directors of
National Consumers League, was confronted with this theory of
the marketplace. She was telling the subcommittee that the contents
of baby food jars were disappearing: "You know that these two
jars of baby food look the same. One contains 4¾ ounces and one
4½ ounces. I do not buy baby food any more. My children are
all grown. But I have a little grandson and I know my daughter-in-
law spends a large part of the food budget on baby food. I am not
at all sure that she knows that one of the brands contains one-
quarter of an ounce less than the other. I am going to tell her about
this."

Whereupon Minority Counsel Dean W. Wallace, who was representing Republican Senator Roman Hruska, suggested that brand
name, not cost, might be the proper basis for purchase. "Do you
think it will make any difference?" he asked.

Mrs. Newman's eyebrows shot up. "To her? The baby will eat
any kind of baby food, and I think the price will make a difference
to her. She knows she has a limited budget. She would rather get
4¾ ounces than 4½."

Mr. Wallace, fearful that he had been misunderstood, elabo-
rated: "I am talking about the brand she is buying. I do not know,
and this may not be the case, but maybe she would buy that same
brand even if she knew there was a difference."

"I hope not," retorted Mrs. Newman. "She is an intelligent
girl. I cannot believe she would. Since the baby will eat either one,
why would she buy the most expensive?"

At this, Mr. Wallace revealed where his idea had come from.

"Dr. Dichter, who was here yesterday," he explained, "said all this would not make any difference. . . ."

"Dr. Dichter" was Ernest Dichter, president of the Institute for Motivational Research. Of all the motivational researchers who testified at the hearings, Dr. Dichter was probably the one with the greatest horsepower. A native of Austria, with a Ph.D. in psychology from the University of Vienna, Dr. Dichter had been a pioneer in motivational research and its application to selling goods. He had given up a private practice as a psychoanalyst in Vienna to come to the United States in 1938. He immediately set about to adapt the clinical techniques of psychoanalysis to the measurement and manipulation of consumer desire. He had become consulting psychologist on programming for CBS. His best-known book was titled *The Strategy of Desire*. In 1940, *Time* magazine had pictured him as "small, neat, emphatic." Now, in 1961, he was larger, heavier, but no less emphatic.

In his graceful Viennese accent, Dr. Dichter fascinated his listeners at the packaging hearings with his proposition that the United States had entered what he called a "psychoeconomic era." According to Dr. Dichter, the psychoeconomic consumer is unconcerned with the quality or the price of his purchases. "What people actually spend their money on are the psychological differences, brand images permitting them to express their individuality," he stated. All products are of high quality, so the consumer does not have to worry about quality. "We have reached what I, in my book, call a psychoeconomic era. It is because of the improved quality and reliability of our merchandise that we can allow ourselves the luxury of making our decisions on the basis of more purely psychological factors.

"Unfortunately, I must report," Dr. Dichter went on, "that about the only label that a consumer ever reads is the content and proof on the liquor bottle. . . . The real problem lies in the fact that the consumer is not as much interested as we assume.

"Sure, the size and ingredients should be listed prominently," he continued, as though humoring a not-too-bright pupil. "Yes, for God's sake, do it. The only thing I try to introduce into this hearing is the public will still not look at it."

Senator Hart was incredulous. "Do I understand you to say that if the content was on there to be easily seen and, to go one step further, in mathematics easily understood, that it would still be a 'do not bother me' type of thing as far as most shoppers are concerned?"

"Well," replied Dr. Dichter, "as the researchers report, unfortunately, yes."

Minority Counsel Chumbris, the voice of Senator Dirksen in the hearings, appeared also to be of the psychoeconomic school. At one point, housewife Sarah Newman, whose testimony about baby food jars had raised the question of brand-name loyalty, held up two bottles of well-known brands of soft drinks for the members of the subcommittee to see. "Here are two cola bottles that are quite interesting," she told Mr. Chumbris. "Do they look the same size to you? I would really like an answer, because otherwise I do not know what to say next."

Mr. Chumbris conceded that the bottles looked to be about the same size.

"All right," said Mrs. Newman. "This bottle has 12 ounces. This bottle has 16 ounces."

Senator Hart asked the witness to indicate where the contents appeared on the bottles.

"That is a very interesting thing," Mrs. Newman replied. "I would like to show you. . . . You see, there is no label on that which you can see. . . . The contents actually are pressed in the glass, then the dark liquid is put in, and let me tell you, the light here today is much better than it is in a lot of supermarkets. But you try. I think you gentlemen would be interested in seeing how difficult it is to get the reading there."

Senator Hart peered intently at the two bottles handed up to him, his long features setting in lines of disapproval. "I think I have not expressed an opinion in the course of these three days that would imply a harsh judgment on any item," he said quietly, "but in my book somebody stayed awake a good many nights to make sure that you and I were not sure of what we were being offered. . . . I ask Mr. Chumbris if he would not agree."

"The only comment I make on that," replied Mr. Chumbris,

"is that this bottle has been an established bottle since I was a little boy. I never cared how many ounces were in this particular bottle as compared with this one because if I bought this particular product, I bought it because of what was in this particular bottle, irrespective of the price or the content. . . ."

The minority counsel was displaying a loyalty to brand that is the mark of the well-disciplined consumer, a loyalty that results in complete disregard for price. Later in the hearings, he and Mrs. Newman went over the same ground together, this time on the subject of cake mixes.

With the air of a teacher in a classroom, her spare figure erect at the witness table, Mrs. Newman held up three boxes. "Here are three packages of fudge brownie mix," she lectured. "The two smaller ones on the shelves look pretty nearly alike, although one is actually thinner and a little longer. This thinner one, which is longer across this way, contains 15½ ounces. The other smaller one contains a full pound. You would naturally expect the bigger one to contain more. Instead, this has only 15½ ounces in it."

The handsome minority counsel, a graduate of Georgetown Law School and former assistant attorney general of the State of New Mexico, attempted patiently to explain the theory of cake baking to the Washington housewife. "Mrs. Newman," Mr. Chumbris said slowly, "when a housewife or the husband goes to the market to buy a box of cake mix, she is buying a box of cake mix that will make a certain cake to her specifications. So if one box is a little bit bigger than the other, it wouldn't really make any difference to her as long as she gets the particular product that she wants from the particular company because it is going to bake a certain type of cake. In other words, one box isn't going to bake a cake and the other going to bake a cake and a tenth. Each of them is going to bake a cake irrespective of the size of the box, isn't that true?"

It must have been something of a shock to Mrs. Newman to realize the level to which the discussion had fallen. It appeared that it was now necessary for her to make the point that not all cakes were the same size. Gamely, she went ahead. "Cakes are baked in different sizes," she informed Mr. Chumbris. "Not all cakes turn out to be the same size. If you put more ingredients in, you are very likely going to get more cake."

To which there could be no reply, and Mr. Chumbris made none. Instead, he threw out a cloud of black ink and retreated from the field. "But as I understand it from the testimony and talking to the people who are in this particular business," he replied, "when they put up a box now which is much different than they did 10 or 15 years ago when a housewife did much of the work herself on that, now they give her a box, she dumps it into the pan, adds whatever it says on the box, and shoves it into the oven, and they make that cake with a certain amount of ounces. Whether it is fractionated or not, it bakes her a specific cake and if it doesn't she will change to another company the next time.

". . . Mrs. Newman, you and I had some interesting colloquy the last time you were here and they are in the record there, they are part of the record. Much of the matter you have discussed has been discussed by other witnesses and there have been witnesses who have disagreed, so in the final analysis we will just have to evaluate your testimony as against other testimony and come to a decision on it, and because of the time, I think that I will pass."

In yet another discussion with Mrs. Newman, Mr. Chumbris appeared to suggest that the way of salvation for the shopper would be to patronize the small corner grocery store if she wished to be treated fairly. Somehow, he seemed to imply, she had brought all this trouble on herself by patronizing the big supermarket. Mrs. Newman was telling the subcommittee about her difficulty in determining the price of cookies.

"Here are two packages of chocolate chip cookies," she indicated. "Somebody has been nibbling away at one. But they look pretty much the same. One brand contains 7¾ ounces. This one has 8½ ounces. If the price were different, 27 and 29 cents, to divide 7¾ into 27, and 8½ into 29—well, I do not know. You shop all the time, Mr. Chumbris. Could you do that quickly? Could you find out which is cheaper?"

"I have made it my business to check those things," the minority counsel replied. "I may not do it on the spot. If I do not do it at that moment, I will have it figured out for next week."

But Mrs. Newman was not to be deflected. With cool aplomb, she pinned down the elusive Mr. Chumbris: "I think you will agree that it would be difficult and time-consuming to do that right there when you are faced with picking one box of chocolate cookies."

Mr. Chumbris succumbed. "I agree with you on that point." He then escaped into irrelevance. "That is why I say we get back to these large chainstores rather than this small store on the corner. The consumers brought that on themselves. They could still go to that corner store if they wanted to."

Mr. Chumbris agreed there was a problem. His solution, apparently, was to return to the days when cookies were shipped in barrels, which were opened by the grocer and left to stand in his store for days or weeks, while, day by day, he reached in by hand to fill brown paper bags and weigh them out, a pound at a time, under the watchful, suspicious eye of the purchaser.

Roy King, editor of *Food Field Reporter,* defended fractional net weights on the grounds that the calculation of weight per ounce was a simple one that any housewife could perform without difficulty. "We suggest," he said, lapsing into the editorial first person plural, "that the housewife . . . should be expected to take the time to divide fractionalized weights into fractionalized prices in order to determine the 'best buy.' It is a very simple process and can be easily done. I shall be glad to demonstrate it at any time."

No one on the subcommittee took advantage of the educational opportunity. Mr. King went blandly ahead.

"Many manufacturers, and some of the largest, on all of their products put the net weight in close proximity to the price so that the women can calculate the price per ounce or the price per pound."

Staff Counsel Cohen remained unconvinced. "If she can calculate," he said doubtfully.

"Well," replied Mr. King, with some heat, "I mean, you insist 'if she can do it.' My kid is in the seventh grade and she can do it."

Mr. King's kid should have attended the session during which

Mr. Chumbris and the subcommittee's economist, E. Wayles Browne, Jr., ran into some difficulty in comparing the prices of detergents. Dr. Browne had done some shopping in a Washington supermarket and had come home with four different sizes of the same detergent. He had bought the "home laundry" size, 16 pounds 1 ounce, for $3.99; the "king" size, 5 pounds 3¾ ounces, for $1.31; the "giant" size, 3 pounds 1¼ ounces, for 79 cents; and the "large" size (the smallest of the four), 1 pound 4 ounces, for 33 cents. Dr. Browne testified that he had used a calculating machine to determine that the four sizes cost, in order, 1.553, 1.564, 1.604, and 1.650 cents per ounce. He concluded that "the home laundry, the big economy size here, is a little bit cheaper per ounce than each of the preceding sizes."

Mr. Chumbris: Did you figure the percentage on that?

Dr. Browne: I did, sir.

Mr. Chumbris: Seven and a half per cent?

Dr. Browne: A fraction over 6 per cent difference between the smallest and the largest size.

Mr. Chumbris: I figured 7½.

Dr. Browne: You go into a slide rule, please, and you will find—

Mr. Chumbris: I took the difference of 155 to 165, which is a difference of 10, and 10 against 165 is about 7½ per cent.

Dr. Browne: You are doing a pretty good job of approximating an answer, and if you say it is around 7 per cent, I shall not argue with you. If you say it is over 7 per cent, I say it is less than 6½ per cent, because I ran it on a calculating machine.

Senator Hart: I think the point that is being brought out is that it just is not that we are slow at arithmetic in a supermarket, but it is a tough job.

Dr. Browne: You cannot divide a four-digit figure into a three- to five-digit figure and get a four-digit figure in your head.

Mr. Chumbris: The only trouble with that is that the housewife is a little smarter than we think she is. She will take that home laundry size and take it home, because she is going to go back in a week or two and get another box. She is going to figure out that 7½ per cent difference. That is right. Do not put the housewife in the class of a moron, Dr. Browne, because she is not going to be that way.

Senator Hart: Wait a minute, you are reflecting on the chairman here.

Mr. Chumbris: No, I do not mean to.

Senator Hart: You are, because you are implying that if I am unable to do that computation in my head, I am a moron, and that is nonsense. This is a very complicated operation.

Just which side walked away the victor in this exchange was debatable. But a reading of the record does very little to support the contention that the average housewife could easily perform such calculations. Later, during the Commerce Committee hearings, Senator Maurine B. Neuberger of Oregon and John M. Cowan, the managing director of the National Flexible Packaging Association, failed one of these simple arithmetical exercises. The senator and Mr. Cowan each held a package of chocolate-covered peanut clusters, of different brands. One was marked 6¾ ounces for 33 cents, the other was 7¼ ounces for 39 cents. The senator asked Mr. Cowan which package was less expensive.

"I would say they are awfully close together if I were a shopper," replied Mr. Cowan, apparently unable to perform the calculation. "I would not worry about the ounces. If I like the Kraft name, I would probably buy this." Mr. Cowan was evincing the disdain for price that is the mark of the faithful consumer. "You have the choice of buying [the other package] if you prefer," he told the senator. "That is the marketplace."

The choice that Mr. Cowan had in mind was apparently the choice between two brand names. This was not without its merit, but Senator Neuberger would have preferred to know the price as well.

Other defenders of the status quo deplored the emphasis on price implicit in the Hart bill proposals. Price, they seemed to argue, was a relatively unimportant factor in buying decisions. Quality, value, and other less tangible attributes were of great significance, and to give the shopper information about price that was too explicit would do him a disservice by drawing his attention away from these more important attributes. A manufacturer of glass jars and bottles told the subcommittee: "We think it extremely unlikely that even ounces would materially aid the consumer in making price-per-ounce comparisons, in the light of prevailing pricing practices at the retail level; nor would it greatly benefit her if it did, for such comparisons leave out consideration of differences in quality and a multitude of other factors which enter into her concepts of value."

Scott Paper's Harrison F. Dunning, who earlier in the hearings had quietly wondered at the number of consumers who count the sheets in a roll of toilet paper, echoed the fear that the shopper's system of values might be distorted by explicit information about price. "Another thing about sticking this price per unit on the label," he said thoughtfully, "is that it tends to make price the one yardstick on which you buy, and I don't feel that is right. I think that price is only one of the elements. The quality, the value, the utility, and all those things are elements, too. I think to emphasize price per unit would tend to emphasize price as your basic consideration in making a purchase, and I am sure that you men don't do that. . . . We shouldn't encourage the consumer to make price her only yardstick because value and quality and those things are very, very important aspects of this."

No advocate of the Hart bill denied that factors other than price should enter into the buying decision. They did maintain, however, that price should be one of the factors, and they contended that the consumer was being denied the right to know the price.

But the food merchants stubbornly refused to face up to this charge. They preferred, instead, to pooh-pooh the importance of price in making a purchase. Typical was the testimony of J. Arnold Anderson, vice-president of Safeway Stores. "[As to] odd-size packaging, particularly the use of fractions making it difficult to make price comparisons," he stated, "based on our experience as retailers we think this has been overemphasized as a 'problem.' . . . We feel that the customer's free choice is preferable to any arbitrary delimitation of package sizes or regulation of certain full or fractional ounces of net contents. . . . We submit that fractional ounces in large packages have very little effect on cost per ounce calculations or other, more typical customer assessments of comparative values. We believe that cost per ounce (or any other precise measure of weight or volume) is seldom the sole or paramount criterion of value to the customer."

Some manufacturers resisted giving consumers specific price information on the grounds that the esoteric nature of their products rendered price entirely meaningless. An employee of the Colgate-Palmolive Company told the subcommittee: "Some of those who have appeared before your committee would lead you to protect the consumer against imagined depredation by standardizing sizes and other devices under the erroneous assumption that a fluid ounce of any of several shampoos or face creams is equivalent. Nothing could be further from the truth. For example, most shampoos are aqueous solutions of selected synthetic surfactants. Unless you are prepared to control the type of ingredients and their concentration which constitute a shampoo—in other words, unless you are prepared to dictate cosmetic formulation—the control of net contents is no more meaningful in protecting the consumer against unscrupulous trade practice than it would be to dictate the size of a book or the length of a play or motion picture."

From "aqueous solutions of selected synthetic surfactants" to Shakespeare and Otto Preminger was apparently a leap in values taken easily by the soap manufacturers. An attractive woman spokesman for the cosmetic producers led the subcommittee even further into the mystical, make-believe world of toiletries. "Cosmetics and toiletries are not household commodities," she told the committee. "They are not standardized, utilitarian items subject to gages of specifications on some common denominator of performance with other work-a-day products for the home. Makeup by definition is an artistic device. Fragrance by its very nature defies specification and standardization. Cosmetics are of glamorous stuff. To specify a standard container, to stultify the label with unnecessary conformance to utilitarian uniformity would destroy the glamour, precipitate the whim and dissipate the dream."

Pretty heady stuff. Rather difficult for a mere male to cope with. But on reading this testimony in the newspaper, one woman dissented. "I am sure you were not taken in by the nonsense of packaging and labeling regulations 'precipitating the glamour and dissipating the dream' of cosmetics," she wrote the subcommittee, with a pleasing disregard for strict accuracy. "I enjoy pretty pink bottles as much as any young wife and mother, but buying a tube of lipstick for $2 in which the lipstick takes up only one-third of the tube does not make me feel particularly feminine."

Or, as Jerry Cohen put it, once he had regained his wits: "When you hear 'a little dab will do you,' you may want to know just how many little dabs are in the bottle."

One of the more baroque arguments against the standardization of net weights was put forth by Mrs. Sylvia Schur, president of Creative Food Service, Inc. Mrs. Schur had been food editor of *Woman's Home Companion, Look,* and *Seventeen.* Her position apparently was that net weight markings on packages were unnecessary because she could make an accurate estimate merely by eye. Senator Hart asked Mrs. Schur whether she felt it would be useful to have the net weight marked on the wrapper of a bar of soap, a requirement not part of existing law.

"I tell you," replied Mrs. Schur, "it would do me very little good, I believe, to know its weight in some instances. It depends on the quality of the soap and the purpose to which it is to be put, whether it is a hand soap and includes a certain proportion of cream in it, or whether it is a laundry bar of soap or a strong soap for scrubbing."

"Suppose there are five sizes of Ivory soap," the senator persisted, "would it be helpful to you in making a rational judgment to know how much it weighs?"

"I can see that pretty well," said Mrs. Schur.

The senator was incredulous. "I am amazed at your answer. Really, I am. You, who would teach home economics, to have doubt about the usefulness of knowing how much each of five similar products, identical products, weighed in order to make a price comparison. I am amazed at that."

"But, Senator," Mrs. Schur protested, "if they are the same product and they are next to each other in the supermarket, it is almost faster and easier to look at them and see. Certainly if the weight was stated and I wanted to take the time to compare them on my product, that is fine."

Senator Hart was stymied. He could only conclude lamely that he and Mrs. Schur must be of different species "because my eyes don't measure weight."

The accumulating testimony from the opponents of the Hart bill was providing a picture of the average housewife-shopper that some were finding difficult to comprehend; she could perform complex long division rapidly in her head, and she could accurately estimate the weight of an object by sight; but on the other hand, she never read labels, made most of her purchases under the spell of some dream-like emotional impulse, and cared not a whit for price.

It was probably with some sense of relief that the subcommittee turned its attention from the peculiar attributes of this infantile superwoman to more solid questions. What, for example, would be the effect of the Hart bill on the economy as a whole? Suppose the continual shifting and shuffling of package sizes, shapes, and net weights were to be tempered by standardization?

The witness from Colgate-Palmolive who had earlier introduced the sobering phrase "aqueous solutions of selected synthetic surfactants" into the testimony, predicted economic calamity. "Never lose sight of the fact," he warned, "that the constant change in graphics and form [create] employment for many thousands who design and make new molds, new plates, new dies, new mechanical layouts, new inks, new models, new artwork, and so forth. Thousands would lose their jobs if size and shape are arbitrarily controlled. Changing the bottle and cap design of a major toiletry product can provide up to 1,000 man-hours of employment. To curtail this activity could drastically reduce employment in the industries which serve our business."

This was a pure exercise in sophistry. Neither the Hart bill nor any of its advocates called for any controls on package design, except that it be nondeceptive. Standardized net contents in some product lines, yes. But those who maintain that this would result in drab package uniformity need only to examine the shelves of a liquor store, especially during the Christmas season. Every bottle contains just a fifth of a gallon, but the variety of design seems infinite.

The loudest and most persistent cry against the Hart bill was, in the words of the National Association of Manufacturers, that it would be "an unwarranted intrusion by the Government into normal marketing practices." Not only did the proposed standardization of package contents place a yoke on the neck of the free-enterprise businessman, it restricted the free choice of the consumer and imposed unwanted conformity on society. "The biggest crime being perpetrated in this bill," said Senator Dirksen, "is the fact that more Federal regulation is being espoused over both the manufacturer of the packaged goods and the consumer, who desires to obtain a greater variety of packaged goods in the quality, quantity, and at the price he chooses to pay. Stifle this freedom and the consumer may have to go back to the horse and buggy days of consumer goods but at higher prices. The time has come when the Federal government must stop this philosophy that it and it alone can determine what is best for management and for the consumer."

These sentiments were echoed by Senator Hruska. The Hart bill, said he, "divests the consumer of his right to dictate the details of the products he buys and gives that right to a Government bureau. This being done, the producers' rights are automatically destroyed since they are contingent upon the expressions of a free purchaser. . . . What qualities does government possess which justify this invasion of the rights of the constituents of the free enterprise system? Has it some mystical power which enables it to look into the minds of people to determine their wishes? Has it a unique ability to make sound business judgments?" The bill, he went on, "is an economic, not a consumer protection bill. It legislates against variety—not deception. In the eyes of its sponsors variety is an evil thing. It is evil because it means consumers have a number of products to choose from. According to their view, this sort of abundance makes shopping a difficult and burdensome chore because the shopper must make selections from the many items displayed to him. . . . The pernicious conduct of a few [producers] should not stampede us into enacting legislation the focal point of which is not deception but suppression of the right of free choice."

Senator Hugh Scott of Pennsylvania hinted that the Hart bill was part of a larger conspiracy among a certain group in the Federal government to destroy the free-enterprise system and run business from Washington. "I think it is just as well to bring this out from under the blankets," he said bravely. "This is an attempt to put into the Government bureaucracy the operation of American business in this field. It has no health purpose, no sanitation purpose, no safety purpose, and it has been so testified. What other purpose does it have? Economic control. And that is what they are after. And this is one step, just as you have other steps, all of them are given nice names like truth in this or truth in that, all of the rest.

"There is no truth in this truth-in-packaging bill. This bill is a bill to fix standards to control industry, to make government supreme, and to provide a great many additional jobs down here, which industry has to presumably pay for and which the housewife will pay for, because you would pass all of these costs on, I am sure."

Many industry representatives and trade associations repeated this charge. The Premium Advertising Association of America stated that the bill "involves a truly dangerous encroachment on the freedom of advertising and of competition. It is the conviction of this association that advertising and sales promotion should remain free of arbitrary control because such freedom best insures a competitive market and makes for a prosperous economy."

The National-American Wholesale Grocers' Association stated that "enactment of this legislation is unnecessary, potentially dangerous to the food industry and to the whole concept of free American enterprise. . . . Any attempt, under the guise of promoting honest packaging and labeling, to restrict the right of persons engaged in packaging and labeling consumer goods to engage in lawful pursuit of business through ingenuity in packing and merchandising is an unwarranted and dangerous extension of Government control of private enterprise. . . . The philosophy behind this type of legislation strikes directly at the individuality, initiative, and inventiveness which has made our food industry the envy of the entire world. To saddle it with the yoke of mediocrity achieved through standardization requirements dictated by Government regulatory agencies will provide a totally unnecessary burden which can only hinder and impede developments and improvements which the consumer has become accustomed to receive from the food supplier and food merchandiser."

A long parade of businessmen to the witness stand repeated these sentiments. William R. Tincher, vice-president of Purex Corporation, spoke for them all when he told the committee: "The complete standardization of product and package by the government is a burden of an enslaved people whose government has decided that people are stupid, that it knows better than they what they shall need and shall have."

The sentiment was not a new one. Fifty-five years earlier, when attempts were being made to pass the first Pure Food and Drug Act and introduce a semblance of control into the wild, perilous jungle of Kickapoo Indian Sagwa, Galvanic Love Powders, and Dr. Bridgman's Electromagnetic Ring for Rheumatism, three members of the House of Representatives investigative committee signed a minority report on the proposed law that read, in part: "We challenge the right of Congress to enact such a law as this. It occurs to us to say that this is but another effort to minimize the power of the States and to magnify the powers of the General Government, in an effort to look to the General Government for the correction of all of the ills and evils from which the public may think it is afflicted."

Regulation by government has always been resisted by those being regulated. And quite naturally so. But as the small, individual businessman and shopkeeper has given way to the giant corporation and the "chain" retail store, and the economic and political power of the producer and the vendor has overwhelmed the defenses of the consumer, it has become necessary for government to assume the role of arbiter in the marketplace, to protect the consumer from the rapacious producer, and to protect the free, competitive market from debasement by unfair and predatory methods of competition.

Still, there were those in industry who seemed to feel that the Hart bill would have the opposite effect. R. Allan Hickman, an employee of Dow Chemical Company and vice-chairman of the All-Industry Packaging Advisory Committee, stated that the bill "would so bind industry as to injure competition."

Senator Hart confessed that he had always had some trouble accepting fully the sweeping proposition that his bill, if adopted, would injure competition. If in fact every member of the product line was required to observe the same ground rules, he asked Mr. Hickman, how would that injure competition?

Mr. Hickman's reply was reminiscent of presidential press conferences of an earlier decade. "It would be difficult," he said, "without being terribly specific, in an industry such as detergents— and I can't speak for the detergent industry—and, therefore, I can only refer to my statement that sometimes in attempting to standardize different densities of materials we could, in effect, cut down the amount of money that was spent in research to produce a lighter weight package, a better package, because the standardization of the package itself might prevent that package from being in competition with other packages of products that were either of less quality or were of a different density."

Apparently somewhat uncertain as to the meaning of that reply, Senator Hart returned to the subject a moment later. "I am wondering what specifically in this bill do you regard as injuring competition if, in fact, everybody had to abide by the same standards?"

Mr. Hickman tried again: "Excesses of competition would be a case in which the same product, having to appear in exactly the same sized package, exactly the same weight, might in that rare case—but which does happen, and which is responsible for your interest in this bill—involve the use of adulterated materials which would, in effect, make it weigh the amount that it was required to weigh, be the same size that was required to be, and yet at the same time would not be in fair competition."

With that, Senator Hart abandoned the line of questioning.

For ideas, it is necessary to turn once again to the testimony of Roy King, editor of *Food Field Reporter,* who had attested to the skill of his seventh-grade kid in computing prices. It was during these Senate hearings that Mr. King elucidated what may be called King's Theory of the Volumetric Society.

"I would like to point out," said Mr. King, "to a large extent, this is what we like to call a volumetric society, and it calls for volumetric advertising. By volumetric, we mean that the consumer views a given product in terms of volume usage, rather than avoirdupois weight. Although net weight, by pounds, ounces, pints, or gallons, is included on the package because the law so decrees, the consumer views his purchase by so many cupfuls, so many servings, or so many teaspoonsful. As a matter of fact, just about every cookbook in America will bear this out. If you care to examine any representative cookbook, you will see that the recipes are in cups and half cups, and in measures of that sort.

"The housewife is buying performance and service, in terms of usage, not by weight, necessarily. Fractional weights are actually of minor significance, when compared to product performance. Should food firms attempt to package all of their products in standardized weights or sizes, sometimes, the quality would suffer, because formulas must be developed freely, without regard to ultimate package size or weight. Which is preferable?"

One of the pitfalls awaiting the proponents of the volumetric society can be envisioned by recalling the case of the inflated shortening; in 1960, when Lever Brothers began to whip nitrogen gas into Spry to increase its bulk, housewives found, to their dismay, that there was less shortening per cupful than there had been. The moral of this is that a pound is a pound is a pound, but a cup is subject to negotiation.

The treachery of volumetric thinking was further illustrated in the testimony of motivational researcher Edmund W. J. Faison. Dr. Faison, it will be recalled, had earlier instructed Senator Hart in the mystique of slim salad oil bottles vis-à-vis calorie-conscious housewives. "There are two processes for making instant potatoes," Dr. Faison pointed out. "One is known as the granule process and the other is the flake process. Now, if you dry your potato and make it into a series of granules you can get it in a much smaller container than you can if you slice the potato into little chips and dry them. This takes more room."

Dr. Faison then pointed out that a box of the "granule" potatoes would be much smaller than a box of "flake" potatoes, since the flakes were much less dense. "But the important thing to the consumer is that both of these will give eight servings of potatoes even if one does weigh a lot more or a lot less than the other." Dr. Faison nearly reached home base safely. What he meant to say, of course, was that the two boxes *weighed* the same. Because of a difference in density, it was the *volumes* of the boxes that were quite different. Which illustrates the dangers of volumetric thinking.

Further elucidation of the volumetric society was offered by Minority Counsel Peter Chumbris, who made use of the theory to explain the fractional weights of detergent packages. In the witness chair was Donald Lefever, grocery manager for Greenbelt Consumer Services, who had earlier informed Mr. Chumbris that 64 ounces was a half gallon, and who had aroused the ire of the minority counsel by impugning the motives of the food manufacturers.

Mr. Lefever testified that on a recent trip through three supermarkets in Washington, he had found 180 brands and sizes of detergent packages. He observed that one brand was offered in four sizes: 20, 49¼, 83¾, and 257 ounces. These odd numbers, he said, would make it very difficult for a shopper to calculate the price.

Mr. Chumbris saw nothing wrong with this. "Now, do you have any objection to a housewife who has eight children buying a detergent that is 257 that you dictated here?" he asked. "Is that right? 257? If she so chose? Or if it is a lady who lives in an apartment alone and she wants to buy a box with only 20 ounces, you are not going to deprive her of that privilege under our American competitive system, are you?"

"I don't think I made any inference in that direction," replied Mr. Lefever.

"You point out that there were too many sizes," Mr. Chumbris charged.

"I don't think I said there were too many sizes. I said I thought there should be a more logical—they should come in more logical multiples. . . ."

"What is so objectionable to these four that you mentioned?" insisted Mr. Chumbris, sweeping aside logical multiples. "One is 20, the other 49, the other 83 and the other is 257."

Jerry Voorhis, executive director of the Cooperative League of the USA, who had accompanied Mr. Lefever to the witness stand, broke in here. "I would like to say what I think is objectionable. Why not give them 1, 2, 3, 4, and 5 pounds or something like this so people could compare the price of one brand with the price of another. . . ."

At this, Mr. Chumbris invoked the volumetric society: "Mr. Voorhis, now I would say if that could be brought to a logical conclusion by the manufacturer, you would have a point there, but the manufacturer comes here and tells us that he manufactures his detergent according to certain washings. The wife needs 4 cups or 5 cups or 8 cups and when they put these cups in, it might come out to 49.2 ounces. And this is his explanation."

In other words, what the housewife *really* wanted was to buy detergent by the cup, not by the pound, because she *used* it by the cup. So the manufacturer designed a box to hold exactly 20 cups, because if the housewife came to the bottom of the package and had only a half cup left, she wouldn't know what to do with it. It just so happened that 20 cups weighed 83¾ ounces. This argument, although barely able to support its own weight, was not strengthened by the fact that the directions for use on one leading detergent package were to "use ¾ to 1 cup for full load of normally soiled clothes," and for "heavily soiled clothes or extremely hard water, use slightly more." Following these directions, the housewife was still likely to be left with that perplexing fraction of a cup at the bottom of the box.

On the question of the much-maligned detergents, J. Gibson Pleasants, vice-president for research and development, Procter & Gamble Company, began his testimony with the statement that "a comparison of cost-per-ounce is meaningless." His reasoning: different detergents differ widely in their cleaning efficiency. A pound of detergent "X" packs a much greater cleaning punch than a pound of detergent "Y." Further, he said, an emphasis on weight of product might "have the detrimental effect of encouraging product debasement—the introduction of inert, or bulk, or weight-building additives." The manufacturer might be tempted to put, say, sand into his detergent formula just to beef it up.

The latter possibility, of course, is always present, whether the weight on the label is 83¾ ounces or a plain 5 pounds. As to Dr. Pleasants's first premise, many of his listeners were more inclined to agree with former advertising executive Nicholas Samstag, who wrote: "All the competing makers [of detergents] tell their half-truths at about the same rate; they all make about equally effective (or ineffective) products so that nobody can do very much about it if the product doesn't live up to the claim."

Some of those listening to Dr. Pleasants recollected the spray-dried sodium phosphate detergent additive, with which detergent manufacturers could inflate their product with air bubbles to increase its volume by 20 to 30 per cent. How long, they wondered, would this be profitable if detergents were priced by the pound instead of by the eyeful?

Jerry Cohen, the quiet-spoken subcommittee counsel, challenged Dr. Pleasants's statement that a cost-per-ounce comparison of detergents was "meaningless." Dr. Pleasants brought to the witness table no mean talents. He had earned his Ph.D. at the California Institute of Technology in 1933. He was a member of the American Chemical Society, the American Association for the Advancement of Science, and other learned societies. He had been in the detergent business for thirty years. In the ensuing questioning, Mr. Cohen declined to debate detergent quality, but he did pursue Dr. Pleasants relentlessly and skillfully on the "meaningless" cost per ounce. It was the youthful lawyer versus the experienced scientist.

Mr. Cohen: Mr. Pleasants . . . the tone of your statement indicates that at least in the detergent field you feel that the cost-per-ounce comparisons are meaningless. Is that correct?

Dr. Pleasants: Cost-per-ounce alone. Taken in combination with other information they could take on meaning, but cost-per-ounce alone could be quite confusing.

Mr. Cohen: I'm sorry. I was just reading from your statement where you say: "I must respectfully submit, however, that this provision of the bill will not accomplish its goal because in the case of most manufactured goods, a comparison of cost-per-ounce is meaningless." Would you care to modify that?

Dr. Pleasants: No. I am quite content with the statement as it stands because the other condition, namely, the availability of other information about the product, is normally not easily available to the consumer.

Mr. Cohen: How many sizes of Tide do you have, for instance?

Dr. Pleasants: I would hazard a guess that we have about four. That is not strictly precise, about four sizes.

Mr. Cohen: If the consumer is not able to determine the price-per-ounce, how is she going to determine which of your various sizes of Tide is the best buy for her?

Dr. Pleasants: I don't think she could determine it without being able to effect such a calculation.

Mr. Cohen: Then at least insofar as determining which is the best buy between the various sizes of the same product, net weight would be extremely meaningful for the consumer, would it not?

Dr. Pleasants: That is correct. They can be in conjunction with price where you are talking about the same product in all sizes. That I yield to you on.

Mr. Cohen: By the way, how do you buy the ingredients for these products yourself? On what basis? I mean the chemicals that go into it?

Dr. Pleasants: On a tonnage basis. Pounds, tons, and so forth.

Mr. Cohen: You want to know the quantity of these.

Dr. Pleasants: Price per ton, price per pound, yes.

Mr. Cohen: Shouldn't the consumer have the same opportunity to make this kind of comparison, to buy on a price-per-ounce in the smaller amounts if she wants to?

Dr. Pleasants: We have no desire to prevent the consumer from being able to work out a cost per unit weight, figure it for herself. We are apprehensive of overweighting that as a consideration in her mind through special markings, through the hue and cry that goes with a new set of rules. . . . Therefore, we in fact work out this sometimes difficult arithmetic for her in advance, as a matter of fact. I submit the further thought, however, sir, that those who wish to deceive, that distribution among human nature who wish to deceive, will retain that appetite I think under any set of rules. . . .

Senator Hart: You would not want us to say, would you, that the absence of the information that enables that woman to make a comparison in your Tide reflects an untruthful, dishonest manufacturer?

Dr. Pleasants: No. We would not.

Senator Hart: This is the trouble we have in these hearings. What we are talking about is this middle area where the information that is absent would be helpful, as you have already conceded.

Dr. Pleasants: Mr. Chairman, excuse me. The information is not absent on Tide. It is simply a little difficult to calculate, I think. The information is absent on some of the toilet products. And to attempt to complete a rather subtle thought about a change of rules, I submit that those who wish to deceive among us manufacturers will probably retain that appetite under even new rules. . . . .

Mr. Cohen: Of course, if you make some of these practices unlawful, the appetite may still be there but it might be more dangerous to partake of forbidden fruit.

Dr. Pleasants: Don't forget the diluents, sir.

Mr. Cohen: Let us talk about that for a moment. As I understand your basic point, it is this: If you made price-per-ounce comparisons too easy, it would tend to downgrade quality considerations. Is that your basic point?

Dr. Pleasants: I don't think it will, Mr. Cohen, in the mind of any reputable and conscientious manufacturer who are the ones that make up the great, great majority. I am mistrustful of the refocusing of emphasis, however.

Mr. Cohen: On price as opposed to quality?

Dr. Pleasants: On price per ounce, and I am mistrustful of the hazards of misleading the housewife by a new set of laws, the publicity that goes with it, price per ounce is from now on easily calculated, everything is going to be simple from now on. . . .

Mr. Cohen: I agree with that. But it will be just a little easier

than it is now. The housewife would have a little better chance
than she has now.

Dr. Pleasants: To make her own calculation, yes sir.

Mr. Cohen: Suppose a woman uses [two detergents] and dis-
covers that one is twice as effective as the other. Isn't price-per-
ounce still important to her so that she can determine whether the
one that is twice as effective is not three times more expensive?

Dr. Pleasants: I agree, sir.

Mr. Cohen: I only want to establish the point that price-per-
ounce can be meaningful in this soap opera.

Dr. Pleasants: Mr. Cohen, the last thing we want to put for-
ward is that price-per-ounce to the consumer is of no significance.

The staff counsel had brought the vice-president a long way
from "meaningless."

That there was some validity to some of the arguments brought
against standardization of package contents there could be no
doubt. Many housewives *are* careless about reading labels. Their
loyalty to brand to the exclusion of other shopping information,
infused by a lifetime of exposure to brand-name advertising, is a
strong element in their shopping decisions. The symptoms of the
"psychoeconomic era" and the "volumetric society" are unmistak-
able. Housewives, in short, are not entirely rational buyers.

Also, as has been noted, in some products, such as canned soups,
variations in density of the contents of uniform-size containers
result in fractional weights that are unavoidable without either an
economically unreasonable profusion of package sizes or a resort
to partially filled containers. This provision of the Hart bill was
not intended to apply across the board to every item in the supermarket. As Senator Hart said: "Reasonable weights or quantities
could be set under the bill, but only on a product-line basis and
only after a host of safeguards are met, including a finding of
necessity, compulsory consultation with industry, plus hearings,
and judicial review. This section obviously would have only
limited application to correct some of the absurd market situations
uncovered at hearings. The bill has nothing to do with sizes or

shapes of packages, except those that are deceptive, and everybody agrees those should be driven from the marketplace."

But all other arguments fade beside the proposition that the shopper deserves to be told, in easily understood terms, the price. To deny him this is to deny him information that is essential to the rational operation of a free market. The food manufacturers themselves demand nothing less from their own suppliers. But, as one witness told the subcommittee, the food manufacturers are operating under a double standard: "Manufacturers do not buy raw products for processing by the declaration of bags full, bins full, trucks full, carloads full, piles, stacks, or tankloads. . . . Manufacturers buy on grade differentials, and they buy by the foot, the pound, the gallon, or integral parts thereof. . . . They package to meet competition and consumer preference with full knowledge of unit content. If they are proud of their product, they should be equally proud to conspicuously declare how much the consumer receives for the price paid. To do otherwise is to evade fair practices."

8

What Is a Serving?

A housewife in Chicago, browsing through her supermarket for a dessert to give her family that evening, picked up a can of pear halves. There were four in her family: herself, her husband, and two teen-age boys. The label on the can said, "Serves approximately four." Although the can looked a bit small to hold four servings, she shrugged her shoulders, threw the can into her basket, and moved along.

That evening, at dessert time, she opened the can and dumped the contents into a bowl. There, at the bottom of the bowl, submerged in a watery juice, were exactly three pear halves. With clenched teeth, she put the three halves into a saucer for herself and went to the freezer to get ice cream for the rest of the family. Had she divided the pears four ways, each member of her hungry family would have received ¾ of a pear half, or ⅜ of a pear. Later that evening, she sat down and wrote a scathing letter to the manufacturer. She was as indignant as though her purse had been stolen.

On many of the labels in the supermarket—canned fruits, frozen foods, desserts, for example—the manufacturer, in an effort to be extra helpful to the shopper, includes information as to the number of "servings" in the package. "Serves 6" or "3 to 4 servings," the package says. No doubt many housewives, being creatures of the volumetric society, are unsure how many pitted cherries there are in 15½ ounces, and the manufacturer's statement as to the number of servings in the can helps her to decide how many cans are needed to fill her family's stomachs.

The question is, how big is a serving? One man's feast is another man's appetizer. The housewife can gage her family's appetite against an average, or a standard, provided there is such a standard. But there is not. It seems a serving is just what the manufacturer says it is, no more and no less. To one manufacturer, a serving of peaches might be two halves; to his competitor, it might be one half or three halves. It is like buying by the hatful—and using the seller's hat as a measure.

The Hart bill proposed to set a standard. Section 3(c)(4) provided that, whenever servings appeared on the label, the Food and Drug Administration could issue regulations to "establish and define the net quantity of any commodity (in terms of weight, measure, or count) which shall constitute a serving. . . ." Information about servings on the label is perfectly fine, said the supporters of the bill; indeed, it can be very helpful to the housewife. But only if some disinterested agency, such as the Federal government, defines the size of a serving. Without such a definition and such a standard, listing the number of servings on the label is more harm than help, since the housewife is at the mercy of each manufacturer's private definition of what constitutes a serving for his own product.

Senator Hugh Scott seemed to find this idea ridiculous. "On this business of servings," he announced, "to attempt to have the Government decide what constitutes a serving of food reaches, in my opinion, the Annapurna of asininity, if you want a phrase for it. A hamburger serving for a person of 17 is very different from a hamburger serving to a person of 70. . . . It would be simpler to just have the housewife run in and ask the postmaster how much she should serve of this and that for a household of five and, presumably, it would be invalid to represent you could serve five, if some agency said you could only serve four."

Testimony by the opponents of the Hart bill was not always notable for the use of rigorous logic. But perhaps in no other area of contention was the use of the *non sequitur* more blatant. As reconstructed from the statements of the food manufacturers, the argument went something like this:

1. There is no such thing as a "standard" consumer with a "standard" appetite. Stomachs vary.

2. Since there is no standard appetite, it would be impossible to define a standard serving.

3. However, information on servings is useful to the consumer.

4. Therefore, the manufacturer, by extensive study and tests, determines the size of the "average" serving for his product, and this is what appears on the label.

After circling this path several times with several different witnesses, Senator Hart and committee counsel were smiling politely through clenched teeth.

That reform was needed was apparent from the incensed writers to Consumers Union. One housewife said that she had bought a large can (1 pound 14 ounces) of plums as a dessert for her family of five. The illustration on the label showed a bowl containing five plums, and the statement said "6 to 7 servings." The implication was strong that each serving was about five plums, and 6 to 7 times five equaled 30 to 35 plums. From the size of the can, it was obvious that it could not hold as many as 30 to 35 plums, but, if the information on the label was even a half truth, the housewife felt she could reasonably expect to serve five. At dessert time, she opened the can and found just 11 plums—two apiece plus one up for grabs.

Another irate shopper wrote: "In a one-pound can of . . . peeled tomatoes I have found one whole tomato and a small piece of a second. The remainder of space and weight being juice. Now how does a supposedly reputable company . . . have the audacity to state in bold letters on the label—"Servings three to four."

Audacity? Not at all. It was the manufacturer, and he alone, who was the final arbiter on what comprised a serving. If the man who put the tomatoes into the can stipulated that a quarter of a tomato, or 20 grams of tomato, or $\frac{3}{16}$ ounces, was a serving, then it was so. As Scott Paper's Harrison F. Dunning said: "I would say that the manufacturer who makes this product ought to know more about [defining a serving] than anybody in the world, and you could set up any kind of consumer council you wanted to and I don't think they would know as much about it no matter what they did as the guy who makes the product."

But a few sentences before, Mr. Dunning had said: "I have no quarrel with having the number of servings on a package. The only quarrel I have is with anybody trying to set himself up in judgment as to what is a serving." By "anybody," Mr. Dunning presumably meant anybody but the manufacturer.

When it was suggested to Mr. Dunning that all manufacturers of tomatoes might, with the help of the FDA, agree on the definition of a standard serving for tomatoes, he replied: "This would imply that all of us have standard sized appetites and use standard amounts of various products as a serving and, in general, conform pretty carefully to some form of set pattern. This, of course, isn't so. One family will serve dessert portions of twice the size of another family, and I think manufacturers who indicate serving portions on their packages try to the best of their ability to select the average."

This kind of reasoning would seem to argue that gasoline manufacturers, for example, are forcing motorists to conform to a set pattern by marketing gasoline by the gallon. Perhaps the manufacturers should make an exhaustive study to determine the average gasoline consumption for the average car, and the average length of the average trip, then proceed to sell gasoline by the "trip." Three trips for a dollar. Less conformity for the consumer. More freedom for all.

Mr. Cohen made a valiant effort to pin down the elusive Mr. Dunning: "I think the thrust of the testimony to date is or has been that where servings are a meaningful unit, it would be more meaningful to the housewife if servings in one package meant the same thing as servings in another package of the same item so she would have some measure of comparison in terms of how much she is getting."

"Well, that may be so," the paper company executive replied, "but we have got a guy in our office who is a Jello nut. He takes two servings of Jello every noon, has for 25 years. What is the serving going to be for him as against me, and I am not particularly happy about Jello. I will eat it if it is put in front of me, but I am not going to go out of my way to get it. What is the difference? If I have a little serving, I am pretty happy. He has to have two."

Mr. Cohen suggested to Mr. Dunning that, appetites aside, it would be beneficial to the consumer if the Jello box claiming four servings held the same quantity as a competitive pudding also claiming four servings.

It was as though Mr. Dunning had not heard. "Yes," he continued, "I would like to say this, though. Take the product Jello. Everybody in the world has taken a potshot at Jello. . . . Jello sells in portions of servings, as I understand it, and by golly, they go merrily on their way no matter what anybody else is doing. No matter how they designate it, this seems to be what the housewife wants."

And, it appeared, the two men in this dialogue went merrily on their own way, each without regard to what the other was saying. It made one wonder whether they were speaking the same language.

The more the waters were stirred, the murkier they became. Paul S. Willis, the cherubic president of Grocery Manufacturers of America, told the subcommittee that it would be as difficult to establish a standard serving as it would be to regulate tastes and appetites. "Any set of rules or definitions," he stated, "would create considerable confusion in food shopping and food preparation where the housewife is very experienced and very knowledgeable."

Unable to comprehend this hypothesis—that the creation of rules would result in confusion—Senator Hart questioned Mr. Willis further. "Why can we not agree that there should be a standard?" he asked. "When I see marked on the label "one serving," I know that means X amounts of whatever is in it, instead of guessing whether the fellow who drew the label has the same kind of appetite that I have."

"Well, I do not know," Mr. Willis ruminated. "I said here somewhere there is no such thing as a standard consumer, so what would suit you would probably not suit somebody else."

Lines of frustration grew in the senator's lean face. "I agree," he said, "and that is the whole point of this. Why do we not have a label that meets a standard definition of one serving or two servings?"

But Mr. Willis was off again and running. "All I can say, Senator, is this: The food manufacturers are engaged in a very highly competitive business with one another, and they are all catering to serve the consumer. These companies have many departments. They have consumer service departments with very capable women in charge, and they are responsible to find out the likes of consumers. As a result of their communicating with consumers and getting their reactions, they must have concluded that it was servings that they preferred rather than to buy it by the ounce."

Surely this was one of the most unresponsive replies to be offered by any witness during these long, tedious, and often frustrating hearings. But Senator Hart drove gamely ahead, like a man drowning in molasses who realizes calmly that furious activity can only lead to exhaustion and disaster. "Well, now," he went on, "use this as a specific example. If I am a fellow who is trying to get by, I put a label on a box of Jello that says 10 servings, and you have been running about the same volume and your label says 4 servings. I say, 'Look, there is not any standard that you can compel me to measure this by, and I have 10 fellows—it just happens they do not like Jello—but this was an adequate number for 10 of those fellows, so there is nothing wrong with this label.' Is that fair competition?"

"I would say it is fair," Mr. Willis said, "if the package is properly marked."

"It is properly marked in big print, and it says 10 servings on it."

"If the consumer is accustomed to buying that by servings, I think it is all right."

Senator Hart shook his head slowly. "To use this phrase that so many of you people love, we are not communicating, because I just do not understand it."

"Well, I do not think we can change the consumer's ideas," said Mr. Willis with expansive irrelevance. "They are individuals, and so long as they like to buy certain items by servings, they will buy them."

Wearily, the senator went through it again. "What I cannot understand," he said, with measured calm, "is how I can go in and look at a label which says 'four servings' and I buy it and you conclude, therefore, that my motive in buying it is because I want four servings. I have not the foggiest notion, if I really think it through, whether that will serve me four times or not, because if I think about it, I know that the X manufacturing company's notion of how much I need for four servings is just as likely to be wrong as is my guess as to the number of the boxcar that is floating by on the railroad track. This just does not add up. It would add up to a precise communication if there was a standard . . . one serving equals such and such."

"I do not think, Senator, that you and I can resolve that here. I think that we have to depend more largely on what the masses of this country like, and what they will buy, and if they buy it, they must like it."

"My point is," Senator Hart replied, "that they do not know what they are buying, and we are in no position to find out unless we have a standard."

"I will not accept that," snapped Mr. Willis. "I think the American women are the sharpest shopping people in the world."

At this, the passion for relevance drained from the senator. "I bet if you had them here and asked them whether they would like to have a standard for these things, the answering yes would blow the roof off."

"I do not think she would fully know what she is answering," said the grocery executive. "You could not ask her a blunt question like that. She wouldn't fully understand the question."

Which must have been one of the fastest turnabouts on record. The housewife had suddenly been transformed, in Mr. Willis's estimation, from the sharpest shopper in the world to a witless fool incapable of comprehending the most elementary of questions. Senator Hart gave up the fight. The questioning was taken up by the committee economist, E. Wayles Browne, Jr., who appeared confident that, through a clear and undeniable analogy, he could quickly lead Mr. Willis to the light of reason. Dr. Browne's hope was to die quickly.

He began carefully, with the air of a patient teacher coaxing a backward child. "We had some discussion that a serving was a serving whether or not the appetite of Senator Hart was the same as my appetite, for example. And we had some discussion that was a little bit inconclusive as to whether a serving should be defined or how it should be defined. You are prepared to go along with a certain amount of precise size indication on non-food items, are you not, such as clothing sizes or shoe sizes? The simple statement that 'this will take care of one pair of feet' is not enough on a pair of shoes, is it? Would not that line be just about equivalent to your statement, or the canned label statement, that this makes six servings?"

Mr. Willis stared imperturbably at the economist. "I do not see the relationship because shoes must fit your feet," he answered.

Momentarily dismayed by the apparent failure of his lucid analogy, Dr. Browne temporized: "Let me ask one more question."

The witness, sensing a quick victory, pressed his advantage. "Do you want to clarify the question?" Mr. Willis asked generously. "I do not understand it. I do not get the relationship."

"I cannot, sir," the defeated economist acknowledged, "so I will let it go."

But for sheer artistry in obfuscation, one must turn to the woman. The witness was Ellen-Ann Dunham, a vice-president of General Foods Corporation, in charge of General Foods Kitchens, whose major responsibility, in her own words, was "to represent the consumer's point of view at our management table." A 1932 graduate of Cornell University in home economics, she was a veteran in the food business. Her hands folded primly on the witness table in front of her, she sat erect and gave her answers clearly. The questioner was the young staff counsel, S. Jerry Cohen.

Mr. Cohen: I . . . understand from your testimony that in certain areas with certain products you consider "servings" to be a very important thing to your consumer, that she have this information?

Miss Dunham: We consider it very important, yes.

Mr. Cohen: And do you consider it to be meaningful information for the consumer with respect to these products?

Miss Dunham: Yes, I do feel that.

Mr. Cohen: Wouldn't it be much more meaningful to the consumer if four servings, for instance, of your competitor's products meant exactly the same thing in terms of quantity as four servings does on your product?

Miss Dunham: Well, I can't speak for the competitor. With us, four servings is what we have found to be average. . . . When we put a serving on a package it is what we have determined is an average serving. We feel that our products are individual, they have their characteristics, and we consider the concentration of a product where it would be used in a meal. All that influences the number of servings on a package. And I don't feel that we can always analyze our competitor and assume that it is going to be used in the same way that ours is, and that it is the same product, because I think the products vary. And that is why you have variances in servings.

Mr. Cohen: Assuming that you have this in substantially the same products, would it not be more meaningful to the consumer if the number of servings on all of these packages of a similar product meant the same thing in terms of the quantity that was inside the package?

Miss Dunham: Do you mean that we might say four servings, about one-half cup each, is that what you mean?

Mr. Cohen: I am assuming that with industry's help and assistance and concurrence standard servings were set up in certain product lines where they would be helpful so that when a person bought a package, no matter what company it was that put it out, she would know that there was the same quantity in one package as there is in another based upon the serving information that she got.

Miss Dunham: I don't think you can standardize servings.

Mr. Cohen: What do you mean by that?

Miss Dunham: Today I may eat a certain amount per serving, and that is my standard for the day. Tomorrow I may eat more. . . . We can get average servings. And that is the basis which determines the amount.

Senator Hart: But I am a shopper, and how do you know what the average is? No one can determine servings, but if the package says five servings, what do I conclude from that?

Miss Dunham: Well, a woman learns by experience what her family will eat. Institution people have learned by observations what an average serving is.

Mr. Cohen: But you do set average servings, based on your experience you set average servings?

Miss Dunham: That is right.

Mr. Cohen: Wouldn't it be more meaningful to a shopper if the average servings on all packages in the same product line were based on the same standard?

Miss Dunham: I think it might be if you could determine it. The problem would be to determine it.

The lady had taken on the Senator and the counselor, and, singlehandedly, she had them utterly confounded. They had chased her round and round the circle and ended by biting at their own tails. It was perfectly reasonable for General Foods to define what it felt to be an "average" serving. To revert to the gasoline analogy, it was as though each petroleum company were to be permitted its own definition of a "gallon." Senator Hart had summarized the situation in words of one syllable: "They do not know what they are buying."

9

The Jumbo Adjective

If the word "serving" is ill-defined, some of the other words used on a package convey no information whatever. To be told that a package is "giant" size is to be told nothing about its size. Indeed, the intelligence conveyed in the message is sometimes negative; the "economy" size is frequently less economical than the simple "large" size.

It was in the area of the jumbo adjective that the Hart bill worked closest to the bone in its attempt to stake out the proper role of the package as distinct from that of the advertisement. Through decades of inoculation, the consumer has acquired a degree of immunity to the superlatives used in advertising. As one witness pointed out, he has learned to discount a certain proportion of what an advertisement claims for a product. Also, there is normally a certain gap in space and time between his exposure to the advertisement and his encounter, as a prospective buyer, with the product itself, a gap which provides for an increase in his store of antibodies.

But, the advocates of the Hart bill argued, when the consumer is face to face with the package at the instant of the buying decision, he is much more vulnerable to seduction. Any attempt on the part of the seller to mislead, misinform, or betray him stands a greater chance of success. At this point, the consumer deserves full information, clearly presented, with a minimum of distracting hoopla. If a salesman were present, the consumer would ask straight questions and expect straight answers. But there is no salesman present. As the packagers themselves were so fond of pointing out, the package itself is the salesman.

Assume a product for which differences in price and quality, among the various brands, are small. Assume further that the most inefficient producer, by the use of meaningless or misleading words on his packages, is able to imply a superiority of his product, and that the consumer responds by buying it. By competitive methods having nothing to do with price, quality, service, or any other attributes of benefit to the consumer, the reward goes to the least efficient producer and is withheld from his more efficient competitor.

Supporters of the Hart bill hoped to rectify this. Section 3(a)(3) of the bill would "prohibit the addition to . . . statements of net quantity of contents of any qualifying words or phrases." The "full 14 ounces" would become a simple statement of fact: "14 ounces." Section 3(c)(3) provided for regulations to "establish and define standards of designations of size (other than statements of net quantity of contents) which may be used to characterize quantitatively the contents." The use of "king size" would be permitted, but it would take on definite meaning. A king-size jar of one brand of mayonnaise would contain exactly as much as the king size of another brand.

It had all started at about the time of the king-size cigarette, and it had swept through the shelves of the supermarket like measles through a nursery. The words "small" and "medium" disappeared from packagers' vocabularies. "Large" was often the smallest package available, and the adjectives soared upward from there. "King" soon gave way to "jumbo," then to "giant," and the epitome was probably reached in "mammoth." Through this rampant elephantiasis, the vocabulary of size was being stripped of all meaning. As one witness told the Hart subcommittee, "This subcommittee, Mr. Chairman, would serve a useful purpose if it did no more than undertake a jungle rescue operation for the English language." One newspaper observed sourly: "Detergents soon may come in four box sizes: regular, giant, colossal, and *full.*"

All very amusing to have a little fun at the expense of the earnest packagers, but the hard question was, Does it really do any harm? Many said yes. It might be one thing, they said, to stomach a certain amount of fluff and nonsense in advertising, which the housewife can read or ignore without loss. But when she stands with cash in her hand, ready to buy, and hoping to make the best buy, there should be a moment of truth. The package should give her the facts, quickly and simply. The package should not serve as a battleground between competitors trying to out-gimmick one another. The simple, hard meanings of "pound" and "ounce" should not be muddied, twisted, or diluted. The standards of weights and measures, evolved by man over centuries at great expense of scientific brainpower, should not be chipped and sullied in the name of competition.

Louis Cheskin, the marketing research and color expert, saw no harm in the use of inflated adjectives. On the contrary, he said, they were "realistic." For the fact of the matter was there was no such thing any more as a small prune.

> The shopper can generally find only giant prunes, colossal or mammoth. I have heard an objection to this. The objector said this was dishonest labeling. He was sure that he was right. He said that the packer should call the three sizes "small," "large," and "very large." On the surface this seems reasonable. Deeper examination shows that it is very wrong. The packager is not dishonest. In fact, the packer is realistic and he uses words that are more meaningful.
>
> When the packer buys the prunes, he gets small ones as well as the other sizes. But, just as the marketer has found that people like "giant" prunes better than "large" prunes and are willing to pay more for "colossal" prunes than for "extra large" ones, he also learned that consumers do not want small prunes at any price. He not only refrains from using the word small, he does not pack the small prunes.
>
> If we start dictating to a packer what kind of words he should use, the next step may be to tell citizens what they can or cannot say and how to say it.

Mr. Cheskin concluded his statement with the opinion that he saw "no need for any new legislation."

But Mr. Cheskin was a reasonable man. In the ensuing questioning, Senator Hart was able to persuade him otherwise. "Is the freedom to use this 'jumbo' and 'giant' and 'super' and all those designations an aspect which you think is characteristic and essential for an affluent society," asked the senator, "or at least with respect to foodstuffs, would it be desirable to eliminate that?"

"In my paper," replied Mr. Cheskin, "in my statement that I have written out, I use olives." (Mr. Cheskin apparently intended to say prunes.) "I had heard an objection that you cannot buy small olives, that you can only buy giant olives and mammoth olives. I put someone to investigate that, and discussed this with a packer of olives. This was some time ago. I asked him, how about small olives? He said, 'You know, we were foolish enough once to have small olives, but nobody would buy them. We get small olives and we have to use them for other purposes; we have to crush them and make other products with them. We cannot sell small olives. We can only sell medium olives, large olives, and extra large olives.' "

Senator Hart asked how the packer had described the three olive sizes, and Mr. Cheskin replied, "large, giant, and mammoth."

But, the senator went on, these words conveyed no information whatever about the size of the olives. Nobody could tell how big they really were. "Would it not be desirable for all of us to know what he is talking about?" he asked.

"Oh, yes," agreed Mr. Cheskin. "There is no debate on that. But you are not questioning, are you, Senator, the use of the word 'mammoth,' or 'giant,' are you? You merely want to define the words 'mammoth' and 'giant,' is that correct?"

That, replied the senator, was precisely what he had in mind.

Mr. Cheskin was persuaded. "I see no objection to defining the word," he said, "but I do see objection to limiting the use of the word."

Senator Hart assured Mr. Cheskin that the only limitation would be to those cases where it told the truth; that is, where it met the definition agreed on. "That is fair enough, is it not?" he asked.

Mr. Cheskin needed just a little more assurance. "By total truth," he asked, "you mean unanimous truth, that would apply to all manufacturers? In other words, there would have to be a

certain standard for the word 'mammoth,' and another standard
for the word 'giant,' is that it?"

"Yes."

"I see no objection to it."

"Do you see any advantage to it?"

"I see an advantage to it."

"Good."

But Mr. Cheskin's pliability was not typical of the opponents
of the bill. Most of them were much more tough-minded. Their
statements in opposition to these sections of the bill heaped scorn
on those who might be deceived by deceit. The use of these
meaningless words on packages, according to Thursten Clarke,
editor of *Food & Drug Packaging,* "could hardly fool anyone but
a fool. They sound good—and all of us like to hear what sounds
good." Acting on this theory, the manufacturer of mayonnaise
should be permitted to claim that his product cures gout. It sounds
good.

Other witnesses before the subcommittee airily waved aside
the abuse inherent in the use of inflated and meaningless adjectives.
Consumers were not confused by them, they maintained, since they
were "obviously used in an exaggerated manner," and "in most
instances these are recognized as the expression of a vendor
touting his wares." Presumably it was all right for the packager to
attempt deceit, provided the consumer was not taken in by it.

As for the occasional housewife who might be deceived, she
was a dunce and ought to know better. For the Federal government
to take steps to protect her from her own stupidity would be an act
of egregious paternalism. E. Lee Feller, the producer of distributor-
controlled food brands who had earlier blamed the packaging-to-
price rat race on the brand-name producers, was adamant on this
point. "Consumers are not children," he said, "and I don't think
they need their movies or their advertising censored of exaggerated
adjectives. We take sensational movies with a grain of salt just as
we view exaggerated use of adjectives by advertising agencies. We
do not cry 'fraud' or 'deception.' As consumers operating within
a free competitive selling and buying structure we need no help
in making a value judgment of exaggerated claims any more than

we need to have censorship of movies that we may reject as in bad taste."

Mr. Feller was "not very much concerned over the use of these 'puff' adjectives." His analogy with movie censorship, however, left something to be desired. Movies, after all, are a nonessential entertainment item. A consumer can go or not go to a movie. And staying home is a very effective form of censorship. Food, on the other hand, is essential to life. And some who heard Mr. Feller's argument were reluctant to agree that the same rules of marketing should apply to both.

A bridge with the world of entertainment was also established by John M. Cowan, managing director of the National Flexible Packaging Association. Mr. Cowan put forth the hypothesis that inflated adjectives should be permitted to appear on packages because of their entertainment value. "What is harmful about a full quart?" he asked. "I do not understand." Anyone who produced a quart bottle of anything certainly should have the option of putting the word "full" in front of "quart." "It is a free word, not trademarked, not copyrighted." As for the word "jumbo," he went on, "I think it is a splendid word. I see nothing wrong with it."

But, Mr. Cowan was asked, wouldn't it be better to have standard meanings for these words? He believed not. "We ought to be able to have a little whimsy left in life."

As in earlier testimony on other aspects of the packaging bill, its opponents made much of the claim that the use of jumbo adjectives was a valuable "marketing tool." For example, motivational researcher Edmund W. J. Faison, he of the calorie-conscious salad oil bottle, protested to the subcommittee that "if you have a particular size that is a special size, if you give it a name it becomes more memorable and in this way it gives you an exclusive. And if I were to develop my full half quart and everybody else has got 12 ounces, 14 ounces, 18 ounces, and 19 ounces, and if I simply throw in one such as 16 ounces, I do not call attention to an exclusive, which may be very important."

Mr. Cohen, who was questioning Dr. Faison, may have wondered to whom it was important. "Could you not," he asked, "just say 'this bottle is 16 ounces'?"

"Perhaps," replied Dr. Faison.

Just what was meant by "marketing tool" was most clearly brought out in the testimony of the redoubtable Miss Dunham, who represented the consumer at General Foods' "marketing table." Under questioning by Mr. Cohen, it became evident that this meant simply that the jumbo adjectives were used to "attract the homemaker's attention."

"In talking to the question of establishing standards of nomenclature such as small, regular, or large," asked the attorney, "I think the objection was that you did not believe it would be practical, is that correct?"

"That is right," said Miss Dunham. "There are so many different products with so many different characteristics."

Mr. Cohen then asked whether General Foods would have any objection to establishing standards, if a practical way could be found to do it within specific product lines.

"I think if we found out that there was a real practical way, we would certainly look into it," Miss Dunham replied.

"Well, more than looking into it, would you have any objections to regulations that would establish uniform nomenclature if this could be done practically and fairly in, say, a given product line?"

"I don't believe that from my experience that it is practical to do that," said Miss Dunham. "And I think it is restricting and limiting the freedom of enterprise, I think there would be some restriction there, because with products varying as they do, with different characteristics and densities, from my own experience, I don't see how you could categorize them into small, regular, or large."

Preferring not to point out to the witness her failure to respond to his hypothetical question, Mr. Cohen took another tack: "You also talk about the problem of super, economy, giant size, et cetera, and I think you based your objection to that on the fact that it would 'unduly restrict entirely proper uses of qualifying or descriptive phrases.' I wonder if you could give us what you consider to be proper use of such phrases, such as super, economy, giant. . . ."

Miss Dunham then defined the proper use of the jumbo adjective: "I think there are cases where a product is packaged, and it is an economy size, and it proves to be so. And it attracts the homemaker's attention to that product, and it is a marketing tool, and if one has conformed to the law and the net contents is clearly and conspicuously shown, if other information is there, it is there for the homemaker to find clearly—this is something of a marketing tool that points out to her perhaps a new product, it is speaking to her from the shelf, it is a marketing tool."

The position of General Foods was clear. The jumbo adjectives were used as a marketing tool to attract the shopper's attention. The words "economy size" were used to stimulate a sale. Since they had no meaning, however, and since, as more than one witness had pointed out, the "economy" size was often more expensive than smaller sizes, they were used not only to convey non-information, they were used to convey misleading information. And that was the way General Foods wanted it. Any attempt to assign meaning to the words would be "impractical." Mr. Cohen pursued the subject of meaning with Miss Dunham yet one more time, and in the end they reached the outermost limits.

Mr. Cohen: You appear to be very much concerned, and General Foods appears to be very much concerned, with giving the consumer meaningful, easy-to-understand information on the labels, is that correct?

Miss Dunham: We try to, yes, and we work at it very hard.

Mr. Cohen: And yet I think there can be no argument that such terms on the label as "super," "giant," "colossal," et cetera, are not meaningful information as far as General Foods is concerned, is that correct? I mean, you defend this on the ground that it is a marketing or merchandising way of gaining customers for the product.

Miss Dunham: And also it is attracting her attention to something that is new that may be useful for her, that is the means of doing it.

Mr. Cohen: But it is not meaningful in terms of describing anything in regard to quality or anything in regard to quantity which is in the package?

Miss Dunham: It can describe a package as being—pointing out to her so that she will recognize it—as being different from the one she used the previous time.

Mr. Cohen: Do you think the use of the word "super," for instance, on the package means something specific to the consumer?

Miss Dunham: Yes, I do.

Mr. Cohen: What does it mean?

Miss Dunham: If I am buying a product, and I—well, let's just be hypothetical and talk about a product that our company might sell—and I might have had a cereal package of such a size, and we have found out that the consumers want a larger package because families are larger, they don't want to have to buy it so often, it is used every day. So we come out, we keep this for the smaller family, we come out with a big cereal package, and we so designate that as super. That is attracting. That is telling me that there is a bigger package there. And I may have been looking for a bigger package. So it means something to me as a purchaser, a homemaker.

Mr. Cohen: If the net weight were there in large letters where everyone can see it on all the packages, wouldn't these superlatives then become unnecessary on that package because she would be able to see the content of the package?

Miss Dunham: If a manufacturer is trying something new, it is a means of attracting her attention.

Mr. Cohen: After the product is no longer new do you still retain the super on the package?

Miss Dunham: No. A new package we consider a new product; by the time it gets into distribution and into channels, it takes about a year before you can be sure that all women know, so we wouldn't keep it on forever.

Mr. Cohen: And after it becomes accepted, then you would take the super off the package?

Miss Dunham: By that time, we might be coming out with another.

Mr. Cohen: What do you call packages larger than super?

Miss Dunham: I don't know what that word is yet.

The final word on the subject of jumbo adjectives should probably be given to Roy Zimmerman, coordinator of packaging for Independent Grocers Alliance. Mr. Zimmerman had told the subcommittee that he disapproved of the use of jumbo adjectives and that IGA did not find much use for them. Whereupon Ronald D. Raitt, who had replaced Dean Wallace as minority counsel representing Senator Hruska, asked Mr. Zimmerman in a tone of sweet reasonableness how he would propose to fill the vacuum produced by the loss of this marketing tool. "It has been developed during the hearings," said Mr. Raitt, "that manufacturers have several different sizes of the product, and this is predicated on the grounds that there are varying sizes of family and frequency of how often the breadwinner is paid. This accounts for varying sizes, and each size possesses its own nomenclature, which we have called superlatives. Obviously, some sort of a handle has to be hung on each one of these sizes. If you object to the use of superlatives, in what manner would you handle this? What do you think would be most beneficial to the consumer?"

"Well," replied Mr. Zimmerman, "following our own practice, we call them a pint or a quart or 3 pounds or 4 pounds."

10

Cents Off What?

An engineer in Philadelphia one Saturday morning was asked by his wife to go to the corner grocery store and buy a jar of instant coffee. When he arrived, he glanced briefly at the shelf display and reached for a jar of the brand they had always used. But as he reached, the corner of his eye was caught by the words "7 cents off" on the label of another brand. The words were in big black type against a yellow background which radiated like the points of stars into the red label. Never one to pass up a bargain, he grabbed the second jar, paid for it, and started home. As he walked, he began to wonder. Seven cents off what? Off yesterday's price? But how could he know what it cost yesterday. Well, then, off the "regular" retail price. But that was surely an unknown number, especially with a product whose price was changing all the time. He reached into the bag, pulled out the jar, and looked at the price stamped on the lid. It said 79. He had paid 79 cents for it. Then the grocer had subtracted the 7 cents before he stamped the jar. Or had he? Not wishing to confess his ignorance of these arcane matters to his wife, he put the jar on the shelf and said nothing about it.

His confusion, however, was justified. To his questions, no one knew the answers. The coffee manufacturer, in printing those words on his label, had made a promise that he could not possibly keep. Manufacturers are prohibited by law to set retail prices. The manufacturer sells to the wholesaler, the wholesaler to the retailer, and the retailer to the consumer, and each at his own price, determined by the cost to him and the markup he wishes to realize. Even though the manufacturer might reduce the price to the wholesaler by 7 cents, there was no guarantee that the price reduction would filter down to the consumer. The words on the label were, therefore, a fraud.

But the cents-off deal was an excellent "marketing tool," so the fraudulent labels permeated the shelves of the supermarket.

In a supermarket in Glenside, Pennsylvania, for example, on April 12 and 13, 1965, the following items appeared on the shelves with cents-off labels: cake mix, cheese, chocolate drink, instant coffee, regular coffee, cookies, pet foods, flour, cake frosting, margarine, evaporated milk, pizza, muffins, salad oil, freezer wrapping paper, pie crust, pie mix, pudding, rice, spaghetti sauce, shortening, potato sticks, soup, spaghetti, syrup, and tea.

Many witnesses before the Antitrust and Monopoly Subcommittee saw nothing wrong with the cents-off deal, either morally or legally. This view was shared by Senator Dirksen's minority counsel, Peter Chumbris. At one point in the hearings, there was a somewhat confused colloquy on the legality of cents off between Mr. Chumbris and Mildred E. Brady, assistant director of Consumers Union.

"You realize that cents off is now legal under our acts," said Mr. Chumbris, "under the Federal Trade Commission Act, and under the Robinson-Patman Act, and the Clayton Act. . . . If they do it in a certain manner it is legal."

Mrs. Brady replied that if it was legal for a manufacturer to promise on the label what he could not deliver, then the law needed to be changed. "Would you tell me how," she asked, "under what circumstances could it be proper for General Foods to promise me 7 cents off on its instant coffee when it didn't know whether I was going to get 7 cents off or not? What circumstances make that right?"

"Well, the point there is this," replied Mr. Chumbris. "Under Section 5 of the Federal Trade Commission Act the retailer who took advantage of that 7 cents off and did not pass it on to the consumer . . . would be prosecuted under the Federal Trade Commission Act."

If Mr. Chumbris was right, said Mrs. Brady, and the abuse of the cents-off deal was indeed illegal, then the government was permitting "mass violation of the law on the part of the food industry" on a scale that would undermine one's faith in democratic government.

Not so, said Mr. Chumbris. It could never happen, because "there is a higher authority than the Federal Trade Commission that would take care of a practice like that, and that is the consumer himself—"

At this, Mrs. Brady broke in with some feeling: "You know, buying goods can be fun and it used to be that spending money was thought to be fun. I would like it to be fun again. I would like to be able, and I am sure every woman who shops would like to be able to take the children to the store with her, to get in there and get out without feeling that she had to watch to keep her pocket from being picked. The consumer does not want to be a policeman. We want to be consumers. We want to enjoy the marketplace. We want to enter it with confidence and leave it without being rooked."

"Well, we are talking about another thing now," answered the minority counsel. "That is another way of life. We can still go to the corner grocery store and take our boy and girl and the man can still dig into the barrel and pick out something. There are still corner grocery stores that cater to that type of business."

What Mr. Chumbris seemed to be saying was that it was possible to receive honest dealing in the small, privately owned store, but that the sign over the supermarket should read "caveat emptor." Which was precisely what all the fuss was about. As to the point about the jurisdiction of the Federal Trade Commission, Senator Hart remarked that it would require an FTC agent in every supermarket to see that the retailer passed along to his customers the cents off promised by the label. And even then, the FTC would be helpless without a knowledge of the "regular retail price" in each store, which was, of course, entirely within the power of the individual store to set.

Section 3(a)(5) of the Hart bill proposed to prohibit manufacturers to place on the package or label of any commodity "any printed matter stating or representing by implication that such commodity is offered for retail sale at a price lower than the ordinary and customarily retail sale price." This section specifically excluded retailers from the prohibition. If the retailer wished to offer cents off, that was entirely within his province. The bill did not prohibit the cents-off deal, it merely barred the manufacturer from promising it on the label. The manufacturer and the retailer would still be quite free to subtract 7 cents from the price, but the pleasure of announcing this to the consumer devolved on the only person who could ensure that the announcement was true—the retailer.

Not only is the cents-off promise on the label an empty one, there is a long history of abuse of the promise. In some products, the labels and the prices shift about so frequently it is impossible to establish a "normal" price from which to calculate the cents off. In other products, the cents-off label seems to be a permanent fixture—a continual markdown from a nonexistent "regular" price.

One man watched the price of Maxwell House Instant Coffee for seven months. In September, 1964, the 10-ounce jar was $1.69. In October, "30 cents off" was added to the label, and the price went down to $1.39. So far, so good. He bought jars of the coffee in December, 1964, and in January, February, March, and April, 1965, and he saved all the jars. They all had the "30 cents off" on the label. The prices varied between $1.29 and $1.59.

A woman in Arlington, Virginia, wrote to the National Consumers League: "For months, the 9-ounce jar [of my brand of instant coffee] sold for $1.59 at most stores, $1.49 at one discount store. Then came the '20 cents off' sale, during which the 'regular' price was stated as $1.89. With the 20 cents knocked off, this brought the price down to only a dime more than I had previously paid. I stopped buying it. The other day, I noticed that the 'sale' is over. At two different markets it was priced at $1.43, with no cents off. I stocked up. I hope I have enough to last me through the next 'sale.' "

A housewife in Barrington, Rhode Island, bought a 1½ pound jar of Ann Page peanut butter for 69 cents. Two weeks later, the words "2 cents off" appeared on the label, and the price was marked 71 cents. A week later, the label read "4 cents off" and the price was marked 73 cents. Each time, the price presumably paid at the checkout counter was the same old 69 cents.

Senator Ribicoff showed the subcommittee two identical cans of coffee. One label said "10 cents off," and the other said "15 cents off." The price marked on both was 59 cents. The two had been in the same store, on the same shelf, at the same time. Cents off what?

One witness told the subcommittee about a product that he had been using for ten years. "They have been selling it in a dollar jar for 50 cents for ten years," he complained. "I do not believe it was ever intended to sell for a dollar."

A reader of *Consumer Reports* wrote to ask whether anyone had ever seen Ehlers Instant Coffee offered at a regular price. He had never seen it without a cents-off blurb on the label. Consumers Union referred the question to the Albert Ehlers Company and was told that Ehlers coffee had been packaged without the cents-off label, "but not so in the last few years." No wonder the Philadelphia engineer was confused. The reason given by the Ehlers Company for the disappearance of the "regular" price for their coffee was "the fierce competition in the instant coffee field."

And so it went. Witness after witness told the subcommittee of similar experiences with various kinds of products. In response to a number of reader complaints, Consumers Union had written to the manufacturers. The replies usually attempted to shift the blame to the retailer. "Once the wholesaler receives our merchandise," wrote Hunt-Wesson Sales Company, "we have no control over the prices charged to the grocer or the shelf price the grocer places on it." Said General Foods: "I'm sure you can understand that General Foods Corporation has no control over retail prices or margin of profit their customers wish to make."

This, of course, was precisely the problem. As one witness concluded, "The branders of most products found on today's supermarket shelves are quite well aware that they cannot control retail prices. Since these manufacturers not only know but repeatedly and publicly proclaim that fact, then obviously, any 'cents off' declarations placed on labels *by such manufacturers* are misleading." [Author's italics.]

Support for the cents-off provision of the Hart bill came from two unexpected sources. One of these was Scott Paper's Harrison F. Dunning; the other was *Sales Management* magazine.

Mr. Dunning, whose earlier testimony about toilet tissue· was memorable, admitted the cents-off matter was a difficult problem. "There has been a great disposition, born of competitive pressure, among manufacturers in the grocery trade in these late years to make cents off the label almost a way of life. The unit keeps changing but the product always seems to have a cents off the label, and it becomes increasingly difficult for the consumers to establish in their minds a fair price for a product which continually has some kind of discount from the label. This is a practice of which I personally disapprove.

"Unless you go to a fair trade system, which seems to be collapsing pretty well in America anyway, the manufacturer cannot designate what price a product is going to be sold for on the store shelf, he sells it to the grocer, and the grocer can sell it at any price he wants to, less than cost, at cost, or above cost. And this, of course, is our way of doing business in America. And so we have no way of saying what the price is going to be in the store."

Scott Paper Company had tried cents-off deals for several years, said Mr. Dunning, but they had given it up. Not only did it fail to increase sales, it increased costs.

"We added to manufacturing costs, because we had to make a special inventory; we are sure the wholesaler and the retailer has extra cost, because he has to withdraw his standard stock while the deal is on and put it back in the warehouse, because it is dead storage, and it ties up space and money, and so on." Mr. Dunning might have added the cost of printing the special packages or labels. His listeners were left to determine for themselves who ultimately paid this extra cost.

The editor of *Sales Management,* which, as Senator Hart noted, "has had some less than laudatory judgments to pass on the Antitrust Subcommittee of the Judiciary Committee," fell in line with the subcommittee in his editorial in the March 15, 1963, issue:

I assume that manufacturers know what they are doing when they print on their boxes and cans "9 cents off." To the best of my knowledge it all started several years ago with one of the makes of instant coffee who marked in big red letters on his jar "7 cents off."

Off what? I asked myself. I couldn't answer. Off what? I asked my wife and several shopkeepers. Nobody gave me an answer that made any sense. I dismissed the matter as being one of those "now-you-see-it-now-you-don't" fleeting market gimmicks, but I couldn't have been more wrong. A competing coffee maker soon stamped his jar "9 cents off" and another made it "11 cents off" and so on.

And the amazing thing (that is, amazing to me) is that it has kept up for several years and spread to many supermarket and drug items. I assume the practice has grown because manufacturers have found that it influences housewives.

In front of me as I write is one of the new "air removed" Kleenex boxes, and on two diagonal corners they have printed "2 cents off." I checked the price of the box at a grocery chain, at Woolworth's, at my neighborhood pharmacy. They were all selling it at the same price. I still have the unanswered question, off what?

Last year an exhaustive congressional inquiry was conducted into deceptive packaging practices, and I am not surprised to learn that Senator Philip Hart introduced on January 21 a bill that would prohibit the printing on packages of cents-off price offers. I don't know that a housewife is actually harmed by such promises, but I wish someone would explain where there isn't at least a mild form of deception involved. How does it differ in principle from the shylock merchant who takes an item normally worth $5, marks it up to $10, then cuts it back to $5 and advertises a sensational half-price bargain?

The ethics of the practice were hammered home by Senator Hart through the stubborn resistance of James E. Mack, lobbyist for the National Confectioners Association. Mr. Mack had testified that he felt the manufacturer "might rightfully presume that if he sells to the wholesaler or retailer a quantity at a proportionally lower value and states on the package the words 'better value,' that he reasonably might assume that it would reach the marketplace in that form."

But to Senator Hart, the presumption of the manufacturer might very well be of little value to the consumer. There was not any guarantee of the truth of his announced "sale" price, was there?

"But by you—" Mr. Mack stammered.

"Is there? Yes or no?"

"Well, I think—"

"Yes or no."

"There is not, no."

"No," the senator concluded gratefully.

In defending the cents-off circus as a legitimate "marketing tool," General Foods' formidable vice-president, Ellen-Ann Dunham, at first suffered a temporary memory lapse or fit of confusion as to just what the practice was. Mr. Cohen had asked Miss Dunham whether she considered it fair and proper for a company that had no control over the price to print on a package a cents-off statement over which it had no control.

"We do not put the price on the package," said Miss Dunham.

Mr. Cohen saw his error. General Foods indeed did not put the selling price on the package, it marked only the number of cents off on the package. He tried again: "You put the 'price off' on the package?"

"Not the amount," Miss Dunham replied. "We only have a little slogan which says, with blank cents off you pay only blank; the retailer marks the package."

Mr. Cohen was at a loss. Scattered on various tables throughout the hearing room were General Foods packages bearing plainly such labels as "7 cents off" and "5 cents off." He had only to appeal to these to demonstrate Miss Dunham's error. Instead, he asked again, "You don't put the amount of cents off on the package?"

"No," Miss Dunham insisted, "the manufacturer doesn't mark the package."

Still unwilling to contradict the lady, Mr. Cohen gently retraced his steps: "I think possibly I confused you a little bit here. I mean on the package you may print 7 cents off."

"No," Miss Dunham denied for the third time, "we don't print the amount off, we will say blank cents off." Then she hesitated, apparently confused. "Are you talking—explain again what you are saying."

Grateful that the awkward moment had passed, Mr. Cohen explained: "Many of your competitors have printed on the package '6 cents off' or '5 cents off' or '3 cents off,' which is printed by the manufacturer on the package." Attributing the practice to Miss Dunham's competitors was surely a gallant move.

"I know what you are talking about now," said Miss Dunham firmly.

"And the manufacturer," Mr. Cohen continued, "has no control over what this final product is going to be sold for?"

Miss Dunham admitted that the manufacturer had no control.

"Do you see anything incongruous or anything wrong in this situation?" Mr. Cohen asked.

"If it is clearly marked on the package," replied Miss Dunham, "and the dealer, the retailer marks it down; no. Of course we have no control over the retailer."

This hypothetical disavowal in response to a straightforward question was unsettling to Senator Hart, and a little later he returned to the question: "Do I understand correctly that General Foods does not sell food products with a label bearing the expression '6 cents off,' '7 cents off,' '5 cents off'?"

Miss Dunham replied that General Foods did indeed produce such packages. "And if I misled you, I shouldn't have."

"I thought the record was a little vague," the senator said wryly. "And yet," he went on, "we are in agreement that you are in no position to insure the fact that it is 7 cents off to the consumer?"

"It is on the face of the invoice," replied the witness, "and we feel that by so putting it there, it is passed on to the consumer, and our experience has been that it has passed on."

"You would agree with us, though," asked Senator Hart, "that this is a practice which properly should be carefully studied, wouldn't you, because there is no real guarantee?"

Miss Dunham agreed that it might be worthwhile to study it.

Senator Hart then asked whether General Foods would have any objection to a legislative prohibition against it.

"I feel that it limits your marketing. . . . It restricts you. . . . It has been a marketing tool, and I think our marketing people have found that it has been beneficial, I think this is the only answer that I can give." It appeared that Miss Dunham's repertoire of equivocation had been exhausted.

Senator Hart's quiet voice assumed an unaccustomed edge: "I have no doubt that it is beneficial to the producers."

A major use of this marketing tool, according to many industry witnesses, was to introduce a new product into the market. This is a difficult thing to do successfully under any circumstances, particularly in the highly competitive supermarket. For that reason, they argued, manufacturers should be permitted to use the cents-off gimmick to launch a new product.

The paper executive, Harrison F. Dunning, was asked how this is possible. How could there be a valid offer of so many cents off the "regular price" of a new product, since a new product doesn't yet have an established price? "That is a darned good question," he replied. "It is a little hard to do. . . . Some people do that. I don't think it is smart."

Many food producers attacked this section of the Hart bill on the grounds that cents-off deals are beneficial to the consumer, that they are popular with the consumer, and that the strictures of the Hart bill would deprive the consumer of freedom of choice and of the opportunity to take advantage of price cuts. "The popularity of any promotion is measured by its consumer acceptance," said Paul S. Willis of GMA. "Cents-off deals have proven their popularity, and the homemakers who like them are entitled to have them. Freedom of choice is basic to our free enterprise system, and a great American privilege which must be preserved. Any attempt to outlaw legitimate promotions such as cents-off would surely meet with mass consumer resentment."

Testimony such as this ignored the fact that the Hart bill did not prohibit cents-off promotions by either the manufacturer or the retailer. It merely would prohibit the manufacturer from announcing the promotion on the label of his package. The housewife would not be deprived of the benefits of cents-off promotions; she would, instead, be given much firmer assurance that the promotion was a legitimate one.

This attempt to deceive the housewife about the provisions of the Hart bill was inadvertently revealed in the testimony of Jerome Greene, vice-president of Alfred Politz Research, Inc. Mr. Greene's firm had been hired by the Association of National Advertisers to take a poll of women shoppers on the subject of cents-off sales. One of the questions the pollsters asked the housewives was: "There was an article in the paper the other day that said Congress is considering a bill that would make it illegal for a manufacturer to offer his product to the consumer on a cents-off kind of sale. In other words, by law the manufacturer could not lower his price and mark the saving on the package accordingly. What do you think about this? Do you think that Congress should pass such a law or not?" Of the 1,402 women interviewed, 63.8 per cent said Congress should not pass such a law.

The question was as deceptive as many of the packages scattered about the tables in the hearing room. The bill would not "make it illegal for a manufacturer to offer his product to the consumer on a cents-off kind of sale." It merely would make it illegal for the manufacturer to advertise his sale on his package. It simply was not true that the Hart bill provided that "by law the manufacturer could not lower his price. . . ." Only the second part of this sentence was true: "and mark the saving on the package accordingly."

In an attempt to reveal this deception and thus to discredit the results of the survey, George F. Clifford, an assistant subcommittee counsel, questioned Mr. Greene about the wording of the question in the survey.

Mr. Clifford: Now, Mr. Greene, there are three sentences here, and I particularly direct your attention to the second sentence . . . : "In other words, by law the manufacturer could not lower his price and mark the saving accordingly." Mr. Greene, is that your understanding of what is involved in the cents-off?

Mr. Greene: I believe so, sir; yes.

Mr. Clifford: Did you write this question?

Mr. Greene: I did.

Mr. Clifford: Mr. Greene, are you aware that this whole matter of cents-off is an extremely controversial one?

Mr. Greene: I am now, sir.

Mr. Clifford: You are now. Now, would you be inclined to look upon your descriptions, your identification of cents-off as a proposed prohibition that the manufacturer could not lower his price and mark the saving on the package accordingly, would you regard that now as an oversimplification?

Mr. Greene: No, sir; not for the survey purpose, I would write it exactly as indicated.

Mr. Clifford: What was the survey purpose?

Mr. Greene: To find out women's opinions about a law to make cents-off sales illegal.

Mr. Clifford: But actually, when you ask a question like this, do you not come up with a public opinion poll on a distorted representation of what cents-off means?

Mr. Greene: How is it distorted, sir?

Mr. Clifford: Sir, I ask you if you would not accept it as an oversimplification, that you bar from it all elements of controversy, and you give to it every favorable element. You say that Congress would forbid the manufacturer from lowering his price, and mark the saving on the package. Do you think that this proposal before the committee forbids the manufacturer from lowering his price?

Mr. Greene: Excuse me, sir. I have not read the bill under consideration by this committee and I cannot speak on that subject.

The witness was testifying before a subcommittee of the United States Senate in connection with a proposed bill, and he confessed that he had never read the bill, a document only fourteen pages long, in very large type. It might have been asked why he was appearing to testify at all, since he apparently had no idea whether his testimony was pertinent.

Jerry Cohen worked close to that question a moment later: "Wouldn't a fairer question really have been, in describing the bill, that Congress would only let the retailer put the lowered price on the package? Do you think if you would have asked the question that way, you would have had the same results?"

"I am not sure we would have had the same answer," Mr. Greene replied, "but could I respectfully suggest that is a different problem and it requires a different survey. I would urge this committee to, and I think I agree with you here now, to consider the question that was asked and the results that were obtained in response to it. The results deal with that subject as that question was put, and not with another subject which you have raised."

Mr. Cohen shook his head in wonder. "May I respectfully say"—he spoke very slowly—"that is the precise subject that we are dealing with and this is what the bill does, and this is just another way of putting the same problem—which I am sure you would agree with—to elicit a different answer. I am sure you would also agree that the answers you get to a lot of these questions depend a great deal on the way you frame the questions that you ask."

Mr. Greene replied that he certainly did agree.

At this point, the irascible Senator Hruska interjected the astonishing premise that Mr. Greene's survey and his testimony were entirely irrelevant to the Hart bill. "If counsel would yield," Hruska broke in, "it was not my impression that this survey made by Mr. Greene had to do with this bill. The question asked by counsel a little while ago was whether if the question were put in a different way it would not bear more accurately on the bill. The testimony is that this inquiry by Mr. Greene was not on this bill nor any specific provision thereof. He was making an inquiry, as indicated in his question. I just wanted the record to show that, that we wouldn't think that, so the record wouldn't indicate that he was trying to circumvent or misrepresent or distort provisions of the bill. Am I correct, Mr. Witness?"

Mr. Greene leaped to the sheltering arms of the senator. "Yes, I agree completely," he said eagerly. "That is why we have practiced such full disclosure here in this survey report, so that the committee can see exactly what we did, what we asked in every respect and can assess the evidence accordingly."

But Senator Hart was dissatisfied. He asked slowly, "Mr. Greene, on page 2 of this study you say: 'There was an article in the paper the other day that said Congress is considering a bill which would make it illegal.' What bill were you talking about?"

The jaws of the trap snapped shut. "We had observed that this had happened in many recent days in the newspaper and—of, sure," Mr. Greene stammered.

Remorselessly, the senator bored in: "Was it any bill other than the bill this committee was considering?"

There was no escape. Mr. Greene was forced to contradict his previous answer and to renounce Senator Hruska. "No," he confessed, "S.387 [the Hart bill] was the bill we had in mind in that particular instance in getting the women to talk."

At this point, Mr. Greene found himself with the embarrassing alternatives of having been less than truthful in stating he had not read the bill or of having prepared and conducted a survey about a bill he had not read. The alternatives were not explored. Instead, the questioning went on at length about the details of the questionnaire and the validity of the results, while Senator Hruska's heavy countenance darkened with annoyance.

Finally, compassion for the witness compelled Senator Hruska to abandon protocol and interrupt the questioning. "Mr. Chairman," he exploded, "I think fun is fun, and I think time is time. . . . We have several other very important witnesses, and if this hearing is going to close tomorrow, it will mean that many important witnesses who are scheduled to appear before this committee because of very extended questions of a highly offensive nature here are being prolonged and prolonged and prolonged. I would suggest we sort of reassess this situation and not believe as some people apparently want us to believe that the testimony of Greene is so damaging to the advocate of this bill that he has to just be picked from every bone that he has, and let's get on with the business."

11

The King Testimony

To readers who have persevered this far, it may have become apparent that there is some bias in this account on the side of the Hart bill. And so there is. In the interest of fairness, therefore, this entire chapter is devoted to the testimony of Roy King, a witness who was unrelievedly and implacably hostile to every aspect of the bill throughout his entire testimony.

First, the biography that preceded Mr. King's prepared statement to the subcommittee:

> Roy King is the editor of *Food Topics,* the Nation's largest supermarket trade journal, and the editor of *Food Field Reporter,* the Nation's leading grocery manufacturer business journal. He is also vice president of marketing of *Food Topics* and *Food Field Reporter.*
>
> He has spent over 12 years on the firing line with his own supermarket which was developed into a million-dollar-per-year volume store. Realizing that there must be more to the outside world than the four walls of the food market, he promptly sold the store, built eight additional stores—thereby completing a shopping center with a 300-car parking lot.
>
> He figured, and rightly so, "I'll let the tenant worry about Procter & Gamble, Lever Bros. and Colgate-Palmolive-Peet, etc. Just let the store operator pay a nice handsome rental."
>
> Prior to opening the market and with a brief interlude for war service with the Infantry, Roy King spent his nights (5 years) in the produce market of New York City.

In addition to his duties with *Food Topics* and *Food Field Reporter,* he is also a permanent consultant for a large Long Island chain and has consulted with [35 grocery, advertising, and marketing associations].

He has also actively consulted with practically every large grocery supplier and advertising agency in America. His articles on merchandising promotion have appeared in over 100 manufacturer house organs as well as in *Advertising Age, Advertising Agency, Food Topics, Food Field Reporter,* beer trade publications, soft drink publications, and State grocery papers of major importance.

His regular column in *Food Topics,* "Shelf Talk," is avidly followed by supermarket operators, manufacturers, and agency executives.

He has recently been awarded the coveted Sylvania Electric Co. award for outstanding service to the food industry.

His work takes him into practically every State of the Union each year where he visits with literally thousands of food operators. He has never believed in an opinion for "opinion's sake" and, consequently, documents pictorially all his facts.

Mr. King began his testimony by offering evidence to show that food prices had been rising more slowly than prices of other goods and services, that food manufacturers were realizing very low profits, and that, despite this, the abundance and variety of foods available to the American housewife were unprecedented. These statements went unchallenged.

He then lashed out at the critics of the food industry. "We don't mind if the clothing firms get markups of 40 per cent on their merchandise. We don't mind that jewelers realize 50 per cent on their investments. We don't mind that the Government, in some instances, has found a method to guarantee a return of 6 per cent to landlords. But we do mind that the Government will not allow the food industry to make a profit, and we do mind that the consumer, the nearsighted, prejudiced, and unthinking consumer, attacks his best friend, the food industry, whenever he can."

Having demolished the government and the consumer with one blow, Mr. King then attacked the advocates of a packaging bill. "Necessity's sharp pinch compels each generation, upon maturity, to cleave from the maternal bosom, and proclaim its independence. This pinch is softened to a love tap by the protectionist concept underlying the packaging hearings, and, in behalf of our American heritage, we question the value of treating the consumer like a child. As one of the spokesmen for the food industry, we question the validity of governmental interest in packaging."

The bugaboo of the fractionalized ounce would be no problem if only the housewife were less nearsighted, prejudiced, and unthinking. "We suggest that the housewife . . . should be expected to take the time to divide fractionalized weights into fractionalized prices in order to determine the 'best buy.' It is a very simple process and can be very easily done. I shall be glad to demonstrate it at any time. These computations involve a grade school knowledge of arithmetic." Furthermore, if the housewife chooses to be irrational in her buying, that is her business. "What this committee fails to realize is that, in a democracy, a citizen has an inalienable right to be different; and, in this instance, the difference is the consumer's deviation from rationality as the foundation of her buying decisions. We are living in a psychoeconomic era [and] we now have the luxury of making decisions based on more purely psychological factors.

"The package's most important function is as a sales influence at the point of sale. . . . Today, advertising and packaging are synonymous. . . . The package contains a selling message." If this is wrong, said Mr. King, then there is something wrong with our whole society, since there is the same deep concern with appearance everywhere. People like first-class travel accommodations, expensive automobiles, good clothes. Even lawyers and politicians wish to appear well-dressed. Is this deceptive or unethical? "We think not. We think, rather, that, in addition to living in a psychoeconomic era, we are also living in a psycholegal and psychopolitical era. In fact, every facet of society is tinged with psychological factors. The façade of complete rationality seems to be gone forever—whether we like it or not."

Mr. King then introduced for the consideration of the subcommittee the concept of the "volumetric society." "I would like to point out," said he, "to a large extent, this is what we like to call a volumetric society, and it calls for volumetric advertising. By volumetric, we mean that the consumer views a given product in terms of volume usage, rather than avoirdupois weight. Although net weight . . . is included on the package because the law so decrees, the consumer views his purchase by so many cupfuls, so many servings, or so many teaspoonsful. As a matter of fact, just about every cookbook in America will bear this out. . . ."

Quality is of primary concern, said Mr. King, not quantity. But, although "the vast majority of food products are of exceptionally high quality today, this fact should not be taken for granted. They have increased in excellence because the marketplace, in a system of free enterprise, is extremely competitive, and survival is the mother of invention. Therefore, what matters most to the manufacturer is the development of a formula for his product which will be of better quality than the other fellow's.

"With the new formula ready for marketing, the manufacturer has no desire to bury it on the back of the package. This is the important news, not net weight or contents. He, therefore, has little regard for the fact that the new product weighs 3⅜ pounds; neither does the consumer. Her main worry is its ultimate performance. Will it bake into a 2-layer cake, 8 inches high and 7 inches in diameter? Will it provide four servings of pie? Will it suffice for 11 loads of wash?"

At this point, Senator Hart, apparently beguiled by the Theory of the Volumetric Society, broke in: "I have hesitated to interrupt and will do it only this once. There are other things that we may want to exchange views on following the completion of your statement. But you have made quite a point here of our developing a volumetric society and the fact that when a person goes in to shop, she is concerned with how many washes the box will produce, how many cake layers it will produce. Why would not the logic of your position lead us to the conclusion that they should price it volumetrically, price it by formula and not by ounces?"

Mr. King reminded the senator that "pricing is not a manufacturer responsibility. This is a retailer responsibility, if I follow your question correctly."

"I am just trying to follow your logic," Senator Hart insisted. "You say that what is the real concern to the consumer is how many washes this box will produce. If this is the significant factor, I take it you tell us it is wrong to belabor this business of trying to make the per ounce an easily computable figure."

"Right," said Mr. King.

"All right," the senator continued. "For purposes of our discussion, let us assume that you are right and we are wrong. Why would not it follow that you should put your price up at $5 for 18 washings, instead of $5 for 18.67 pounds?"

Mr. King chose to be unresponsive. "Again, I would like to point out that you are buying a unit of merchandise that contains 11 washes. You are buying a unit of merchandise that contains an 8-inch cake that will make two layers. You are still buying a unit and the price on the unit is determined at retail, what the consumer will pay for it. The manufacturer does not set retail prices, sir."

Senator Hart replied that the retailer does not set the number of ounces in the package, neither does he mark the label to indicate the number of washings that could be accomplished by the contents. Mr. King agreed that this is not the responsibility of the retailer.

After some additional tail-chasing on the question of who was responsible to give the consumer whatever information he might require to make a rational buying decision, Mr. King moved into the question of where on the package the net weight should appear. The front of the package, he said, should be reserved for the sales pitch. No one had any right to require that the net weight appear on the front. "No one has a right to restrict the manufacturer from making his sale. No one has a right to interfere with the sales message by dictating its package placement."

Mr. King then exhibited a series of slides of photographs he had taken in supermarkets showing the positions of packages on the shelves. As often as not, he demonstrated, it is not the front panel, but the side or the end panel that faces the shopper. "Here, for example," he lectured, "is a typical foil department, aluminum foil. Again, you will notice that the predominance of end labels is showing on the shelf, rather than the front panel of the package. The package has literally got to jump from the shelf into the consumer's shopping cart. That package is the only salesman that the manufacturer has in the supermarket, and he is entitled to sell that package the best way he can. He certainly has to have his brand name on there. He certainly has to have sufficient adjectives on there to induce the shopper to buy the package. She has got to be able to see this at once, and, as I say, it has to be able to literally jump into the basket.

"Here you have a dry mix package. The same problem exists. He has all he can do to point out his brand without other superfluous comments on the package.

"Now here is the front panel of [a cake mix] package. They are always in hopes that they will display the front panel. As you see here, there is a good deal of a selling message on here. This happens to be 5 cents off on the purchase of another one of this manufacturer's products. He needs space for all these things.

"My point in all this is—well, before I get to that, I would like to point this out again; here again, another cents off, and you see with the price spot and the fact that it is 4 cents off, and with the brand name and so forth in the commodity—"

"Who put on that package, the 4 cents off notice?" Senator Hart interrupted.

"This right here? That is the manufacturer."

"Who is selling it in the store?"

"The retailer."

"It is 4 cents off what?"

"You can see exactly what it is," said Mr. King somewhat impatiently, "4 cents off 41 cents is 37 cents."

"Is the manufacturer fixing the price?"

"No, he is not fixing the price, but that is a deal package."

"What does it mean?" the senator persisted.

"It means 4 cents off the regular price that the commodity would normally sell for at retail. In this particular instance, this package usually sold for 41 cents, usually sells for that. The retailer struck that out and put 37 cents, meaning 4 cents off. It is as clear as crystal."

"And contains much the same quality of substance as crystal, in some cases," said Senator Hart. "That is my dilemma."

Mr. King had moved on to his next slide, showing a shelf display of salad dressings. "Here is a profusion of labels. There is nobody selling any one of these particular dressings. That label has to stand out there. We are entitled to an adjective or two, you know. . . . I have a few words on adjectives as well."

"Stay with the content as well as with the adjective," the senator asked.

"Senator, my point in showing you all this, I am trying to be helpful. It is extremely difficult because of the variety of displays that is found at the retail store level to affix net weight in a specific size, you know. It is going to glare out there or stand out there. This is extremely difficult to do. I am not saying it should be in microscopic type. Who is to say, when we have all these conditions existing at retail, over which the manufacturer has no control? I shall be glad to get back to this. I am sure there will probably be some questions about it."

"I appreciate your last topic," said the senator. "You do agree that before that box jumps into the consumer's basket, it should tell her how much it contains and tell her in a fashion that a reasonable buyer can discover, determine, evaluate?"

"True," Mr. King agreed. "Now, I am positively against any such thing as, for example, having a yellow price on a gold background. We admit these things."

"Is not this a proper function for Government?"

"I do not know if so much of it is a function of Government or whether or not we should not self-regulate ourselves."

"That opportunity," said the senator dryly, "was and always is available."

But Mr. King plunged ahead. "Product terminology as to size has been a sore spot, primarily because it has never been fully understood. With the growth of families, and the trend toward shopping only once a week or once every two weeks, it was found that larger sizes were required. Therefore, a company marketed its products in a regular size, then a king size, then a family size, or giant or jumbo size. These terms are generic. . . ."

"Let me ask," the senator interrupted again, "for the record's clarity, what you mean when you say that a jumbo can of something is generic?"

"Let us talk about a household laundry size," explained the witness. "It means in the trade that it will make a certain number of wash loads."

"It has nothing to do with the formula?"

"No, it has nothing to do with the formula.

"It is apparent," Mr. King continued, "that, for the sake of consumer reassurance, the food industry, together with its colleagues in packaging, must initiate an all-out public relations campaign to educate the public as to the mysteries of packaging and labeling. This, of course, can never be the final solution. We must concede that the unethical few have gone far toward damaging our reputation. . . . Nevertheless, we insist that the great majority of these alleged deceptions are either the result of consumer ignorance of the industry or technical difficulties. These problems cannot be solved through governmental intervention, but should be left to self-regulatory procedures on the part of industry. A profusion of laws usually leads to law-breaking; but in a free society, enlightened self-interest by industry will result in prosperity for all."

The foregoing presents the essence of Mr. King's prepared statement. Before going on to the questioning of Mr. King by the subcommittee, it might be instructive to reduce the statement to King's Fourteen Points:

1. Proponents of packaging legislation are protectionists who wish to treat the consumer like a child. The government's trend is toward "Momism."

2. The government's interest in packaging is not a valid one.

3. The consumer is nearsighted, prejudiced, and unthinking.

4. The food industry is the consumer's best friend.

5. It is the consumer's "responsibility to herself" to take a paper and pencil to the supermarket so that she can divide fractionalized prices by fractionalized weights.

6. In our "psychoeconomic era," the consumer has the inalienable right to make irrational buying decisions.

7. The package's most important function is as a sales influence.

8. The "façade" of rationality is "gone forever" from our society.

9. We are living in a "volumetric society."

10. No one has the right to restrict the manufacturer from making his sale.

11. The package has literally got to jump from the shelf into the consumer's shopping cart.

12. Such terms as "jumbo," "giant," and "king" size have caused some trouble because it has never been fully understood that they are "generic."

13. Most of the alleged packaging deceptions are the result of either consumer ignorance or "technical difficulties."

14. A profusion of laws usually leads to law-breaking.

At the end of the statement, Mr. King and Senator Hart exchanged a few pleasant generalities, then the senator led off the questioning: "You read an editorial in this opening statement of yours. Let me read back to you a sentence or two from another editorial of yours. This is one in the July 17 issue of the *Food Field Reporter,* talking about our hearings: 'If any group is to be spanked en masse, it should be our kleptomaniacal housewives who throw stones from their modernistic glass houses while hiding behind their modernistic code of ethics. Honesty begins at home, Senator Hart.' That is a pretty harsh indictment."

"Yes, it is." The witness nodded. "And if I had it to write over again, Senator, I would write it again, because . . . this is a self-service market and pilferage is quite a problem . . . on the retail selling floor, particularly with small-sized packages, no question about this, and it can amount to fantastic amounts of money being lost through being stolen. As a matter of fact, many retailers in many sections of the store will not accept certain products because they are so pilferable. For example, this may be off the subject somewhat, and if it is, please stop me; lipsticks have to be carded. You know what I mean, put on a card so the thing cannot be stolen and put in a purse. We have many, many such examples of that in the supermarkets, where the customer has a kleptomania.

I remember in running my own store, we have a very highly professional man, a doctor. He had a mania for cheese. He used to steal Muenster cheese. There was nothing we could do about it; his wife knew it and warned us about it. But there is no area within the store that is pilfer proof."

"I do not think it would increase the level of kleptomania," observed the senator, "if you told him how much it was that he was stealing."

Senator Hart then yielded to Staff Counsel Jerry Cohen, whose curiosity about the kleptomaniacal housewife was apparently not yet satisfied. "I believe, in terms of this kleptomaniacal statement you did make," he asked, "that one of the reasons you gave for overpackaging was because of this practice, is that correct?"

"I did not refer to overpackaging for that reason," the magazine editor replied. "I referred to overpackaging for slack fill, to account for slack fill, that they were overpackaging in order to overcome slack fill, the amount of vibration that goes from the packaging line all the way down to the store level where the stuff starts to settle. That is what I meant by overpackaging."

"You did not mean to indicate, then," needled Mr. Cohen, "that the so-called kleptomaniacal housewife was any large proportion of the average shopping group?"

"Oh, of course not," snapped Mr. King. "And, frankly, if you do not mind my saying so, from my standpoint, we are a little off base in dwelling on this kleptomania, which is a side issue at this particular point. It exists."

Satisfied, Mr. Cohen moved to another topic. "You mentioned the fact that it is the performance of a product, rather than just the weight, which is often the most important factor. Do you think it would be advisable to require manufacturers to put the standard of performance on the packages, in addition to the weight?"

Mr. King: It all depends on what you mean by standard of performance, Mr. Cohen.

Mr. Cohen: The number of washes in the package.

Mr. King: In many instances, they do.

Mr. Cohen: For instance, in the case of six or seven different products, is there any standard they would all use to determine what is the standard wash?

Mr. King: No; that is because the formulas are different. Some require a cupful, some require a half cup because of the formula.

Mr. Cohen: Is not this kind of information what the housewife needs to make a rational choice in the marketplace?

Mr. King: How are you going to standardize all this, unless you standardize formulas?

Mr. Cohen: Is it possible to set up a standard that so much of a given product will do a standard-size wash?

Mr. King: Yes, in some instances. For product A it might take a half cupful of the detergent; for product B it might take three-quarters of a cupful; for product C it might take a cupful.

Mr. Cohen: That could be taken into consideration in setting a standard for a specific product. Could not that be done?

Mr. King: Yes; but you are dealing with quality here, because manufacturers constantly strive to improve their product. It is a better product than they had the previous year, and so forth. I think this idea, this standardizing of formulas, would be extremely difficult if that is what you are talking about.

Mr. Cohen: No; I am not talking about standardizing formulas. I am saying if a product was tested, by an agency of some sort, and it was determined that this formula and this size had 8 washes or 9 washes or 10 washes, and this is what the manufacturer could be required to put on his package for the housewives' help, would you have any objection to something like that?

Mr. King: It would depend on how it was finally gotten around to. I would be reluctant to say at this point.

Mr. Cohen: Wouldn't this type of thing be helpful to the woman who is trying to act rationally?

Mr. King: It would.

Mr. Cohen: And it would be helpful on all of those packages where the weight was not really as meaningful as the formula itself—

Mr. King: That is right.

The staff counsel had apparently won a major victory. He had persuaded the witness to agree that it would help the housewife if the manufacturer were to tell how well his product did its job. Satisfied, Mr. Cohen moved on. "I think you pointed out," he asked, "that at the present time many packages are being displayed by many retailers by stacking them instead of the front showing. Now, is not one of the reasons for this because of the fact that the packages have been getting so high and so wide that it is difficult for them to stand on the shelf?"

The implications of this question were unflattering to his friends in the food industry, and Mr. King reacted accordingly. "On the contrary. I take grave exception to this. It isn't because the packages are getting bigger and bigger." He continued, with waning relevance, "Many manufacturers, and some of the largest, on all of their products put the net weight in close proximity to the price so that the woman can calculate the price per ounce or the price per pound."

"If she can calculate," said Mr. Cohen.

"Well, I mean, you insist 'if she can do it.' My kid is in the seventh grade and she can do it."

Unwilling to dwell on the King child's mathematical proficiency, Mr. Cohen turned to the matter of cents off. "On this business of 4 cents off and 7 cents off and 9 cents off, or whatever the deal is, this is something that the manufacturer himself puts on the package. How can he possibly know . . . that . . . savings is going to be passed on to the housewife on a retail basis?"

"He does a lot of things besides just mark up a package," Mr. King reflected. "You are talking about a whole marketing procedure. You have got salesmen that go around talking about this 'new' sales event. He has got newspaper ads, television ads, radio ads. Everybody knows that it is a 3-cents-off package or a 4-cents-off package or whatever the case may be. It is the retailer's advantage to pass this savings on to the consumer and 99.9 per cent of all the retailers, of course, follow suit. They are forced to by competitive conditions."

But, Mr. Cohen wanted to know, "Is there any way the manufacturer can know that this is going to be put into effect by the retailer when he puts that on that box?"

"Does he know for certain?" the witness replied. "Nothing is certain, sir, except death and taxes. We all know that."

Implicit in Mr. King's cliché was the admission that abuses could occur in the use of this marketing tool. Mr. Cohen then asked whether someone, either industry or government, should be appointed to eliminate abuses.

"Well, Mr. Cohen, of course, this is a difference of opinion again. I do not think that this situation is bad enough to warrant governmental investigation, because it is not that frequent nor is it that common, far from it. There are a few that do it. But again, they are suffering . . . economically. They are suffering marketwise. This is the reason they are doing it. Sooner or later they are going to run out of money and they will quit doing it."

"Let's go into another area," said Mr. Cohen. "This is the king size and the giant and the super. You say this is used in the industry to show a certain size. Yet, in the exhibits we had in June, on a cross section of detergents, the giant in one case might have more or less than the super in another. In fact, the regular size in one case was far more than the large in most of the others. So is not this type of what you refer to as a 'generic label' simply confusing to the consumer?"

The witness admitted that the use of these terms could be confusing to the consumer. But when Mr. Cohen asked what should be done to eliminate the confusion, he proposed a curious solution. "Let us put it this way," he said. "I think that we have got to leave this to the manufacturers in the detergent field or manufacturers in the cake mix field to get together and let them see what they come up with as a solution for this. Public education is your answer. Better public relations between the packagers, the manufacturers, and the public, as I pointed out here in my address, is the answer to it."

But, Mr. Cohen asked, suppose the manufacturers do not do the job? Then whose responsibility would it be to do it?

"Well," replied Mr. King, "let's cross that bridge when we come to it."

Senator Hart broke in to ask the witness how close we were to the bridge.

"We have not reached there yet, Senator," Mr. King answered.

Nicholas N. Kittrie, minority counsel representing Republican Senator Alexander Wiley of Wisconsin, had been listening to Mr. King's testimony with increasing impatience. He took over the questioning with some zeal: "Mr. King, you raised several questions which are very interesting, but somehow or other I have to make these comments because I think that you are leaving us with a feeling that really it is all the housewives' fault. First of all, she gets there to pilfer, not to buy, and then if she was only rational, she could find the answers very simply because if she is rational, she cannot be really fooled. Then you say that this is a volumetric society and then you, more or less, ask why does she care what the content is; she should really just care how many servings she can get out of it. I do not do a lot of shopping myself, but I have noticed that if you are going to depend on the servings they say you are going to get out of it, quite often you are going to be misled. I have found that different manufacturers, when they say four servings, these are not my four servings. I like to know exactly what is in there, you know. And in the same product I would notice that a serving to somebody may mean 3 ounces and yet to somebody else it may mean 6. In spite of the fact, or whether this is a volumetric society or not, you do have to give somebody who wants to figure out the contents an opportunity to find out what it is, do you not think so?"

"Oh, I believe in consumer dissemination of information," protested the witness. "No question about it. And what constitutes a serving I, frankly, do not know. I am not here to speak for the industry on what constitutes a serving because—oh, I do want to point out one thing, and this is something else. I take umbrage at one thing you said. I wish that a little less emphasis was put on this kleptomania business. This has no bearing on it. Nor did I say that every customer who comes into the store is a kleptomaniac. This is not true. Senator Hart managed to drag this up out of a previous editorial I wrote, but this is—"

"Apparently you were retaliating against the housewife," suggested Mr. Kittrie, "because she came here to complain and you felt, really, that the complaints—"

"I was not retaliating against the housewife because she came here to complain," said Mr. King heatedly. "The housewife has a perfect right to be heard. You forget, I am also a consumer. She has a perfect right to be heard. My wife has certain complaints also, but—would you like her to testify?"

Mr. Kittrie observed that that was the prerogative of the chairman. Whereupon Senator Hart noted wryly that "I tried to inquire, when I read your editorial, if you had consulted Mrs. King."

Mr. King felt that the questioning was straying too far afield. "To get back to your question—what constitutes a serving—this has not been defined. What constitutes a half cup, a full cup, or a cupful? This is also like a pendulum. It swings one way or the other. All cups are not the same size." The food editor seemed unaware that a cup was a standard of measure comprising eight fluid ounces.

Mr. Kittrie turned to another question that had been disturbing him. "During the last hearings we heard some of these psychologically oriented people who said that the typical housewife is irrational, she does not really care, it does not matter, therefore, we are going to help her to be more irrational. You are spreading this further. If we are going to say that the housewife is irrational, that actually she should be under a guardianship, then what you are really saying is that the Government should become more strict in helping her help herself because by our efforts the consumer is not really able to follow a rational method in his purchasing. This is really what bothers me, because if you are going to say that most people are irrational, that they are not going to make their decisions on the basis of fact, then the only answer is, really, some kind of fascism or communism."

"Well, that is very interesting," replied Mr. King, "but I would like to point out one or two things here. Sir, do you go shopping yourself?"

"I certainly do."

"Do you predetermine what you are going to buy before you go into the market?"

"Partially."

"You do not come back with the extra bar of candy or the extra can of sardines or the—"

"There are very few packages that jump from the display case into my basket," said Mr. Kittrie.

Mr. King ignored the wry allusion to the eleventh of his Fourteen Points. "Well, this is the supermarket economy and that is just it. We are there to provide her with an attractive shopping place where she gets convenience and where she gets the finest foods and the finest quality, the finest merchandise that money can buy. And she buys to the tune, as you know—well, the American food bill is—"

"But I think," Mr. Kittrie interrupted, "there is a danger here in accepting the philosophy that our consumer really is so well off that it does not really matter what he gets because whatever he gets he is really getting his money's worth and, basically, he is not rational."

Mr. King protested that he had never propounded such a philosophy. "You are confusing me, I believe—"

"No, no," said Mr. Kittrie. "There is a point [in your testimony] that the quality of the different products is now of such a high level that the consumer can afford to make an irrational decision." (What Mr. King had said was: "in a democracy, a citizen has an inalienable right to be different; and, in this instance, the difference is the consumer's deviation from rationality as the foundation of her buying decisions. . . . Because of improved quality and reliability of merchandise, we now have the luxury of making decisions based on more purely psychological factors.")

"Well," the witness replied, "I just want to point out to you that there are other things that have taken place in our society which create decisions particularly in the supermarket place. These are other things besides the quantity of an item and the net weights. The presentation. It is the decor. It is a million and one things that act to motivate the consumer to buy. This is a free society. This is what we have developed into. What are you going to do? Legislate all this away?"

Mr. Kittrie said there was no need to legislate all this away "as long as you let a consumer get to the basic facts."

"Fine," said Mr. King expansively, "let's educate them. Let's educate them. I am all in favor of education."

Which is probably as good a place as any to leave the testimony of Mr. King.

12

The Consumer

Some opponents of packaging legislation stood on the proposition that the housewife is too smart to be fooled; therefore any products that try to deceive her will be quickly driven out of the marketplace. A soap and detergent man was willing to admit that the housewife might need a little Federal regulation to help her keep the vitamin manufacturers honest "but when it comes to something like soap, goodness, how dumb do they think the housewife is?" A biscuit man stated flatly that "Senator Hart doesn't understand consumers. You don't fool Mrs. Housewife as easily as he believes." A waxed-paper man boasted that "the women of America are smart beyond words, are rarely if ever deceived, and are perhaps the keenest buyers that we have in this land of ours."

At General Foods it was unanimous. Vice-president Ellen-Ann Dunham claimed that, at General Foods, the consumer was "boss." Moreover, she went on, "we credit her with being a very smart boss, indeed, sophisticated as well as intelligent, articulate as well as enlightened. . . ." Chairman Charles G. Mortimer wrote: "I can testify from experience that when it comes to clever buying, the American housewife can give lessons to a Yankee horse trader. She knows exactly what she wants, and she knows precisely what it's worth to her."

According to Scott Paper vice-president Harrison Dunning, this innate shrewdness of the female had a mystical quality: "I don't know what a woman has that a man doesn't. But she has an innate sense about these things that always comes to the forefront." D. Beryl Manischewitz, the wine maker, who testified on behalf of the National Association of Manufacturers, rhapsodized: "Nature provided her and most women with a built-in sense that is a very good competitor of a computer when she is in a store."

The ultimate eulogy to woman's genius appeared in an advertisement by Scott Paper in March, 1963, during the first hearings on the Hart bill. This panegyric, titled "The Original Computer," was published in newspapers in major cities throughout the country and in *Life* and other mass-circulation magazines. It said, in part:

> Somewhere in that head, among the bobbypins, the hair-do, the perfume, and the problems, there is a thing that makes calculations and decisions. This tricky little thinking center is the oldest instrument of progress in the human race; it is never satisfied with today's cut of meat or cut of skirt. Day in and day out, moment by moment over the years, this feminine computer is concerned with one thing above all others: Value. . . . A strange change comes over a woman in a store. The soft glow in the eye is replaced by a steely financial glint; the graceful walk becomes a panther's stride among the bargains. A woman in a store is a mechanism, a prowling computer. . . . At first the whole epic struggle seems no contest. On one side we have this frail creature. On the other side we have her surrounded by some 20,000 square feet of branded canned goods, branded dry groceries, nonfoods, dairy products, and hosts of other items. In the background are the unseen masses of manufacturers trying to bewitch and bedazzle her into buying. But when our girl starts down the aisle, her defenses are massive. Jungle-trained, her bargain-hunter's senses razor-sharp for the sound of a dropping price, our girl is the easy winner almost every time.

Some witnesses before the subcommittee were willing to admit the possibility that even this razor-sharp jungle fighter might be deceived once by some of the packages resting on the supermarket shelves. But, to a man, they assured the subcommittee it would happen only once. Having taken the package home, opened it, and seen the state of things, the housewife would never repeat the purchase. That package, therefore, would disappear from the shelves. The implication here is that it is all right to let the manufacturers try to cheat, because they will never get away with it, at least not for long. The housewife is an automatic policeman.

Is it true? Leaving aside the validity of the ethical basis for the argument, is the conclusion correct? One case in point is worth re-examining: the famous Delson Thin Mint suit discussed earlier. The Food and Drug Administration had seized a package of these chocolate-coated mints in 1959, charging that the packaging was misleading. It contained 25 percent air. The box held 30 mints, but it was long enough to hold 41. The rest of the space was filled with hollow partitions. After three years of litigation, the courts decided against the FDA. As of this writing, *eight years after the FDA seizure,* the package was still being bought by housewives. In the meantime, competing candy makers, once the government had lost its case in court, had adopted the same slack-filled package.

Delson mints are not an isolated case. The supermarket is filled with packages that have been deceiving shoppers for years, a little here, a little there. Tactics shift from time to time, certain practices gain and lose in popularity among the manufacturers, but the result is always the same: planned confusion.

Other witnesses pictured the housewife as a very different kind of creature. In place of the calculating, no-nonsense creature with narrowed eyes and pursed lips, invulnerable to humbug and chicanery, they portrayed her as a giddy, wide-eyed innocent, care-less of value and substance, responding willy-nilly to the blandish-ments of color, shape, design, and innuendo, or to a deep-seated, irrational loyalty to brand. What's more, said food editor Roy King, she had an "inalienable right" to deviate from rationality as the foundation of her buying decisions.

Under questioning by the subcommittee, Miss Dunham of Gen-eral Foods maintained that housewives are not too concerned with the quantity their money would buy. She had testified that house-wives do like to know the number of servings in a box of Jello. She was then asked whether it is as important to the housewife to know that she is getting 16 ounces of cocoa. "From my observations with women," she replied, "I don't believe that they are as concerned about the ounces of cocoa they buy. They are used to buying flour and cocoa in a certain container. They know how they use it. I don't believe the concern is as great."

Louis Cheskin, the motivational researcher who had instructed the subcommittee on the "psychological communication" of the package, was even fearful lest the emphasis being placed on price per pound by the Hart bill proponents might blind the consumer to the greater psychological satisfactions offered by the packaging itself. "Packaging has now become a part of our esthetics," he told the subcommittee, "a part of our culture, a part of our motivation and behavior, which means that the package on the shelf no longer represents a product necessary for survival. . . . Instead, we have over 90 percent of the items representing other things that have to do with what I call products of an affluent society, psychological satisfactions. Because of these psychological satisfactions, I am very fearful about the overemphasis on weights." Mr. Cheskin went on to say that weights and measures were no longer the essence of life "in our kind of a society of abundance." Price, he said, was fourth on the list of four qualities of a product that appealed to the prospective buyer. More important to the shopper than price was the "psychological communication" about the quality of the product, meaning the package, the "visual manifestation" of the product. To put the price, for example, on the front panel of the package would be to "mutilate the psychological appeal" of the package.

The same point was made by the Viennese psychoanalyst turned expert on consumer desire, Dr. Ernest Dichter. Our modern technological know-how has brought us so far, said Dr. Dichter, that all manufacturers of a given type of product have about the same information to work with, the same level of industrial skills in their plants, and are trying to capture the same market. As a result, one brand of gasoline is about the same as any other, a General Electric refrigerator is about the same as a Westinghouse. What the manufacturer produces by his advertising, then, is loyalty to his brand. This must be done by creating the illusion of a difference. In what Dr. Dichter called our psychoeconomic era, "you are just buying labels, the different kinds of colors, the different types of designs."

Where is the truth? Is the housewife a two-legged computer, or is she putty in the hands of Dr. Dichter, ready to reach, glassy-eyed, for the brand with the built-in loyalty? No doubt the average housewife is somewhere between the extremes, with elements of both in her make-up. Her complaint is that the food packagers are making their pitch to the Hyde salivator in her, rather than the Jekyll calculator. Any efforts she might make toward increasing rationality in her shopping are frustrated by the strident hawking in the marketplace. The last thing the food manufacturer desires is a rational shopper.

He has very little to fear. To shop rationally, the housewife would need the impulses of a sleuth, the stamina of a weight-lifter, and the skill of a certified public accountant. Her shopping tools would be a slide rule, a ledger, and work sheets for her calculations. After making her computations to determine the lowest price, she would enter all prices in her ledger so that charts could be plotted later showing changes and trends. Price information in her ledger would also help her determine whether the price of the cents-off items had been reduced, and by how much. Also, her ledger would record how each food manufacturer had defined "serving" in the past, and how this definition had changed from time to time. Words like "economy," "giant," and "king" she would have trained herself to ignore as meaningless. Her weekly food shopping would take all of Saturday, but she would pride herself on 95 per cent accuracy.

No housewife has the time, the energy, or the skill to do a first-rate job in the supermarket. Most of them assume that there are laws to protect them from swindlers and that the market is a rational place. They assume that a higher price means higher quality, the larger size is more economical, the larger package holds more merchandise, "7 cents off" means precisely what it says, and "serves four" means that the food in the package will satisfy four normal appetites.

Granted that we are all susceptible to the contrived ambiguities of the persuasive image-makers, that all of us are swayed by the incessant ballyhoo, whether consciously or not, and that even the most rational of us occasionally buys the package instead of the product, the illusion instead of the reality. Is it not wrong that millions of dollars should be spent to create a marketplace in which rational behavior is difficult, if not impossible? The fact that consumers act irrationally is no justification for playing upon their irrationality.

Any concerted effort to promote irrational behavior cannot be anything but harmful to the public mental health. This is as true in selling merchandise as it is in conducting foreign policy. Nicholas N. Kittrie, Senator Wiley's counsel for the subcommittee minority, reacted thus to the testimony of the motivational researchers: "I honestly am very disturbed at what I hear, because it seems to me that you . . . try to cater to [irrationality], you try to promote it, you try to increase it. You are trying to create illusions in the public mind. . . . I am very concerned about what this does to the public mind, to our population generally. Any society that is going to encourage irrationality among its citizens is going to have difficulty. . . . I am sure that when Pompeii was doomed for destruction, there were probably some market-research men who kept saying that gold-plated bathtubs were very, very good, because they were wanted by the people."

Dr. Dichter saw no harm in packaging "exaggeration." If you label your can of peaches "gorgeous," for example, and your competitor labels his "reasonably good," the housewife will probably conclude that yours are fairly good and your competitor's are poor. She has been "trained by several decades to apply the same psychological disbelief to both statements." Through constant exposure to exaggeration in every walk of life, "we automatically discount 40 or 50 per cent of these statements by advertisers. . . ." Dr. Dichter painted a picture of a jungle-wise consumer: "We are getting smart. We are getting wise."

Mr. Kittrie was concerned about the implied erosion of the English language. "Is there not a danger," he asked, "that if you let these embellishments add up and add up, they become more extreme, and before long you really do not know what is fact and what is fancy?"

"Well, the danger is not very great," said Dr. Dichter soothingly. "There is a limitation as far as the English language is concerned.

There are not very many other words you can use on top of 'gorgeous.' "

Mr. Kittrie was not placated. "But are you not creating a society that is conditioned to all these wild claims and nobody knows what the facts are?"

"Well, that gets us into a very complicated field," said Dr. Dichter.

It does, indeed. It gets us into the questions of whether language, mankind's only tool for rational thought and communication, might be eroded to the point of meaninglessness; whether a whole society, by gradual conditioning to sophistry, might lose the ability to distinguish fact from fable; whether the health and vigor of that society might be destroyed through loss of mutual trust and good will; whether a civilization might suffer a loss of contact with reality which, in an individual, would be diagnosed as madness.

In the microcosm of the marketplace, the bedlam that results from the corruption of language works toward the destruction of the free, competitive enterprise system. The keystone in that system is the consumer, who, by rational selection, rewards the most efficient producer with his purchase. If the means for making a rational decision are withheld from the consumer, he may reward the less efficient producer. The deserving producer is thus harmed, and he finds he must, in order to survive, adopt the methods of his less efficient but less squeamish competitor. The system breaks down. The contest among producers for the consumer's patronage degenerates into a conquest in duplicity.

In the larger arena, mass chicanery can lead to belief in myths and produce a society of dupes. And when a civilization loses its ability to discriminate between reality and illusion, it loses the cement that binds it together, and it loses the ability to defend itself from the forces of dissolution that continually threaten all civilizations from within and without. In the larger sense, the words we use are labels. When they are corrupted, we are helpless.

If "new" means the same old product in a smaller jar, if "economy" means the most expensive size, if "large" is the smallest size available, if a "police action" means a war, if a "people's democracy" means a totalitarian dungeon, if we can no longer distinguish between a civil war and an invasion, how long will it be before "war" means "peace," "victory" means "defeat," and "ignorance" means "strength"?

Freedom of speech, like all of our freedoms, does not imply unlimited license. In any but a perfect society, of course, it will always be necessary to separate the true and meaningful words from the frivolous and deceptive. "But," writes Walter Lippmann, "when the chaff of silliness, baseness, and deception is so voluminous that it submerges the kernels of truth, freedom of speech may produce such frivolity, or such mischief, that it cannot be preserved against the demand for a restoration of order or of decency. If there is a dividing line between liberty and license, it is where freedom of speech is no longer respected as a procedure of the truth and becomes the unrestricted right to exploit the ignorance, and to incite the passions of the people. Then freedom is such a hullabaloo of sophistry, propaganda, special pleading, lobbying, and salesmanship that it is difficult to remember why freedom of speech is worth the pain and trouble of defending it."

13

The Press

Testimony given in the first series of hearings, in 1961, made good copy for the nation's press. Newspapers told their readers that Senate witnesses had called the consumer a "sucker." Headlines cried: "The Grocery Cart Is Being Used to Take Shoppers for a Ride." Cartoons showed a jack-in-the-box labeled "deception" springing from a cereal box. Columnists lambasted the food manufacturers. Photographs showed a United States senator holding up deceptive packages for all to see. Millions saw the packages on television.

The food manufacturers were dumfounded. They were accustomed to much kinder treatment from the press, into which they poured many millions of advertising dollars. So far, the mass-circulation magazines, which, together with television, have the greatest influence on housewife opinion, had not commented. But as the dust of the hearing settled, the trade paper *Packaging* pointed to the clear and present danger: "If we don't smother all this talk about how the consumer is being deceived and cheated, our whole economy will emerge sell shocked [sic]." Further, Senator Hart was now saying that the hearings had indicated a need for legislation, that he was drafting such legislation, and that additional hearings would probably be held on the proposed legislation early in 1963. The food industry gathered its forces for the counterattack.

Some months before the 1963 hearings were scheduled to convene, Paul S. Willis as elder statesman of the food industry, summoned the publishers of sixteen national magazines to "discuss with them the facts of life covering advertising-media relationships." As Mr. Willis modestly told the story later: "We suggested to the publishers that the day was here when their editorial department and business department might better understand their interdependency relationships as they affect the operating results of their company; and as their operations may affect the advertiser—their bread and butter."

After thus making clear to the publishers that the boot was about to descend, Mr. Willis "invited" the publishers "to consider publishing some favorable articles about the food industry instead of only singling out isolated cases of criticism." It would be good business for both the magazine and the food merchant, he explained, for "as the readers turn the pages and come across an interesting article, they will react more favorably to the advertisement and be more inclined to purchase the product."

Rarely has a more brazen attempt by advertisers to dictate editorial content been documented. Did the publishers shake their fists at Mr. Willis and tell him to go peddle his groceries? Did they return to their offices and tell their editors to ignore any such flagrant pressure from the advertisers? The record does not show their reaction, but some months later, Mr. Willis seemed pleased with the results. "We can point with pride," he noted, "to some of the things which have happened since our visit:

"*Look* magazine ran an article explaining the cost-of-living index published monthly by the Government.

"*Reader's Digest,* an article on 'Why Our Food Is a Bargain.'

"*American Weekly,* an article on 'Are Food Prices Too High?'

"*This Week* magazine, 'The Greatest Food Show on Earth.'

"*Saturday Evening Post,* an article exposing food faddists.

"*Good Housekeeping* magazine, on labeling.

"*Ladies' Home Journal,* a series of articles on food.

"*Life* magazine, several institutional ads, and is devoting its total November 23 Thanksgiving issue to food.

"These articles will surely help to create a better understanding of this industry and a favorable public attitude toward it." And what was just as important, concluded Mr. Willis, the articles made the food manufacturers "feel more friendly" toward the magazine publishers.

Two of the magazines whose publishers met with Mr. Willis, *Reader's Digest* and the *Saturday Evening Post,* had earlier commissioned writers to prepare articles on the Hart bill. Possibly as the result of the Willis interview, these articles were never printed.

A search of the *Readers' Guide to Periodical Literature,* plus direct inquiries to nine of the leading mass-circulation magazines, indicates that, after 1961, with the three exceptions noted below, not a single article appeared on the Hart bill or the problems that it deals with.

Of the two major news magazines, *Time* published nothing. The July 10, 1961, issue of *Newsweek* (pre-Willis) devoted nearly a full page to the first hearings, with a cartoon illustrating packaging deception. Since then, complete silence.

In its July, 1962, issue, *Good Housekeeping* reported the results of a survey of nearly 2,000 members of the Good Housekeeping Consumer Panel. The conclusion: "*Good Housekeeping* editors agree with Senator Hart that consumers are entitled to full information about packaged products to enable them to make rational shopping decisions. The editors believe consumers have indicated by this survey, however, that in most instances they are getting such information. Too, our survey indicates that where there is substantial criticism by consumers, it centers on defective package performance and a lack of adequate use and care information, rather than on any 'deceptive' and 'misleading' practice. Finally, women themselves appear to have developed their own way to deal with those few manufacturers who do not give them information they want: they simply buy products which do."

The January 26, 1965, issue of *Look* (post-Willis) ran an article titled "Let's Keep Politics Out of the Pantry," by Charles G. Mortimer, chairman of General Foods Corporation. Mr. Mortimer heaped scorn on those who pictured the housewife as the defenseless dupe of the scheming food manufacturer. "In their attempt to show why the housewife needs more Government protection," he wrote, "proponents of additional controls have created the impression that she is a timid, naive, confused little woman, hopelessly gullible, bewildered by the endless variety of products on the grocery shelves and exposed, as she shops, to the machinations of lurking, profit-hungry figures who dominate the food business.

"This, of course, is utter nonsense. I can testify from experience that when it comes to clever buying, the American housewife can give lessons to a Yankee horse trader. She knows exactly what she wants, and she knows precisely what it's worth to her."

Mr. Mortimer's qualifications as a shopper were made clear to the readers of *Look* by a photograph of him, with Mrs. Mortimer, wheeling a cart through the otherwise empty aisle of a supermarket. No doubt a typical Saturday morning ritual for the chairman of General Foods Corporation.

After charging that some vote-conscious politicians, through "headline-making innuendoes" and "emotion-charged appeals," were endangering the "machinery of free competition" by an intrusion where government did not belong, Mr. Mortimer got down to cases: "By making all packages 'look-alikes' on the shelf," he wrote, "restrictive legislation would stifle innovation and put a halter on an indispensable form of competition: the freedom to bring out packages which are easy to open, easy to close, easy to handle, easy to store." Not satisfied with this absurdity, Mr. Mortimer went on to warn his readers: "We are faced with the grim prospect of having Government officials tell the consumer what products she can buy and what kind of package she can buy it in."

Angered by this flagrant misrepresentation of the provisions of his bill, Senator Hart wrote to Gardner Cowles, publisher of *Look*. The senator pointed out that the aims of his bill had been distorted, and he asked Mr. Cowles for the opportunity to present his side of the case in an article in *Look*. The publisher replied, "I will be interested to see how much attention the general public pays to the subject in the next several months," the implication being that any decision on the senator's request must be founded on the sound editorial principle of high reader interest. Mr. Cowles's estimate of reader interest was revealed by the fact that *Look* bought full-page advertisements in other magazines, including trade journals in the food industry, in which it trumpeted its publication of "this compelling article." Senator Hart, however, was never given the opportunity he requested.

Esther Peterson, special assistant to President Johnson for consumer affairs, also wrote to *Look* as a result of the Mortimer article, offering to prepare a rebuttal. Robert Meskill, assistant managing editor, replied: "We do not plan to hold a 'debate' on this subject, but we do appreciate your offering to engage in one."

As A. J. Liebling once wrote, "Freedom of the press is guaranteed only to those who own one."

At about the time of the Willis interview with the publishers, Senator Hart had sent background material on his bill to twenty-one magazines in hopes of stimulating an article or some editorial comment. In addition to twelve magazines in the grocery trade field, the material went to *Good Housekeeping, Everywoman's, Family Circle, Ladies' Home Journal, Living for Young Homemakers, McCall's, Redbook, National Business Woman, Woman's Day,* and *U.S. Lady.* No articles resulted. One editor replied, "I think the bill is certainly needed but I doubt whether we can mention it editorially."

A statement issued by the Magazine Publishers Association added a heavy tinge of irony to the total magazine blackout on the Hart bill. This association includes in its membership 113 publishers of more than 300 magazines of national circulation—more than 70 per cent of the total magazine circulation in the United States. A copy of the statement went to the Senate Commerce Committee. "The magazine industry," it said, "is an integral part of the communications network of the United States and has provided a key link in the unification of our country by providing information of a public character to our people." The next sentence indicated what was meant by "unification" of the country: "Through the advertising pages of our member magazines, we provide the stimulus and the impetus for much of the consumer purchasing by the people of the United States. Our magazines have played a significant role both in consumer education and information and market stimulus for the products which are proposed to be regulated by the pending legislation—foods, drugs, and household commodities."

The publishers then came to the defense of the consumer that their magazines had "educated" so well: "To assume, as many seem to, that the consumer is gullible and that the marketer is culpable is to make assumptions which are both unwarranted and unfair." Present law is adequate to ensure honest packaging, they said. Also, "The proposed bill is an open-ended grant of regulatory power. . . . There has been no showing that such regulations are needed to protect the public . . . the housewife would be penalized . . . these results would conflict with the consumer's best interests."

The statement ended on a positive note: "Magazine publishers, both in the women's service and general information fields, have been a primary source of information for consumers for many years. We believe that we have contributed significantly to the amount of knowledge available to the public. . . . We believe that the providing of information is a better and more effective approach than that of creating new and unnecessary Federal requirements which would raise market basket prices and inhibit the creation of new products."

With the magazine publishers brought to heel, Mr. Willis turned his sights on the television industry. The occasion was a speech delivered by Mr. Willis at the Eighth Annual Meeting of the Television Bureau of Advertising, in the Starlight Roof of the Waldorf-Astoria, on November 16, 1962, less than four months before the hearings on the packaging bill would open.

In proud and loving detail, Mr. Willis told the television men the story of his success with the magazine men. Then his tone hardened: "I wish that I could say similar nice things about the relationship of our advertisers with television," he said. "Even though the networks receive about 65 per cent of their advertising revenue from GMA members, there is lots to be desired as it applies to our relationship with their top management. We are not aware of any great amount of cooperation which television has extended to us in passing along interesting, favorable information to the public, information such as appeared in the magazine articles. The newspapers throughout the United States publish a great deal of information relating to food prices, food supplies, nutrition, and so on."

Mr. Willis then singled out for praise a recent article in the Hammond (Louisiana) *Sun,* titled "How About a Great Big Hand for Our Food Enterprises?" GMA, he said, had stacks of such clippings from hundreds of newspapers. "In contrast with these favorable items, we have seen some television newscasts where they seemingly took great delight in bellowing out stories that were critical of this industry." Why, he asked, should this be necessary, when there were so many nice things that television could say about the food industry, its greatest source of advertising revenue? "There is plenty of interesting material available about this industry for radio/TV use, and broadcasting such information should create a better public attitude, the advertising would be more effective, and the advertiser would get more for his advertising dollar. It is something," he said, with all the subtlety of a pointed shotgun, "to think over."

The president of Grocery Manufacturers of America then became very specific. "At last year's hearing conducted by Senator Hart's committee on packaging, labeling, etc., the professionals had a field day. Using clever phrases and isolated cases as examples, they charged this industry with offering deceptive packages, slack-filled packages, mislabeling, insufficient labeling, and misleading promotions." What could the food industry do? "We must be sufficiently capable to get our story across to the American people to retain their confidence in us so that they will continue buying our advertised products."

And, speaking of advertising, surely the television men must realize that the food industry was constantly re-evaluating the placement of its advertising dollars. The number of readers, viewers, and listeners reached per dollar was, of course, very important for best sales results. But the food manufacturer, in making his choice, say, between television and the magazines, was interested primarily in what Mr. Willis termed the "net effectiveness of media." After waiting a moment for this phrase to sink in, Mr. Willis concluded: "I close my remarks with a very pertinent question: What can you do additionally that will influence your advertiser to spend more of his advertising dollars with you?"

Apparently, the television men got the message. During the hearings held the following March and April, the packaging bill was mentioned on two NBC shows—the *Huntley-Brinkley Report,* and a program called *Calendar.* But beyond that, according to Consumers Union, television, "so far as CU has been able to find, paid no attention to the 1963 packaging hearings." Further, Senator Hart had been scheduled to appear on several programs, but his appearances were canceled. "I was told the advertisers had objected," Senator Hart explained.

One of the shows that canceled an appearance by Senator Hart was the NBC *Today* show. Three years later, on July 29, 1966, Republican Congresswoman Catherine May of Washington was interviewed on that show by Herbert Kaplow. Congresswoman May told viewers: "What this bill would do, first of all, is to raise the prices of groceries in every American home today. . . . It's a consumer inflationary Federal Packaging Control Bill. . . . I say this is a deceptive label, when you say 'Truth-in-Packaging,' because it is asking us to pay for protection where the need is really not there." The benefits to the consumer would be "higher grocery bills, losing a chance to choose from good varieties, and having some bureaucrat in Washington, D.C., make her decisions for her."

Once again, Senator Hart asked for the opportunity to reply. At first, NBC refused, but, when reminded of the desire of the Federal Communications Commission that each side of a political question be given equal time, permission was granted. Senator Hart appeared on the *Today* show on August 4, 1966.

Mr. Willis testified before the Hart subcommittee on March 19, 1963. At that time, he was questioned at some length about his bullying of the mass communications media. The questioner was Mrs. Dorothy D. Goodwin, assistant staff counsel: "Is it within the normal activities of your position to influence editorial departments of leading publications?" she asked.

"No, ma'am; no, ma'am," the GMA president protested. "We do no lobbying or any work of that kind, or try to influence trade papers."

At that, Mrs. Goodwin read to Mr. Willis a few excerpts from his speech to the television men, and then she repeated the question.

This time, Mr. Willis was somewhat less emphatic: "The answer is 'No'; qualified. When I met with the magazine people, I tried to point out to them that in our opinion there were many fine articles which would have a public and reader interest they might consider taking a look at, like 'Food Is a Bargain.' You mentioned some of them and the magazine people looked at them. They felt that such subjects had a reader interest and they ran the articles. There were no strings tied to it; there were no commitments requested; there was no insinuation that could be construed in any way that their advertising revenue would be affected. The only thing I said was that if they ran articles of this kind, it naturally would reflect very favorably upon the food industry itself, period. Which I think is wonderful. I think it was a big service to the readers to explain the cost-of-living index which the government issues monthly. . . . We had nothing to do with writing the article. We simply suggested some subjects and they thought they were good, so we [sic] used them."

"Well, you point with pride at your accomplishments, Mr. Willis," Mrs. Goodwin observed. "Don't you think that the average person feels that an editorial in a leading publication is a matter of objective reporting rather than the result of industry's pressures on the editorial department in reminders that there was $1.2 billion spent on advertising?"

"No, there was no pressure," Mr. Willis insisted. "You would be interested in learning about cost-of-living index; you would be interested in reading this story. Any time *Reader's Digest* writes an article, there is no industry that can persuade *Reader's Digest* to print anything except what they think is news to its readers. They ran an article on 'Why Food Is a Bargain'—wonderful. I think that is great for the food industry."

Any legislation that is opposed by a powerful segment of industry has a tough row to hoe unless it can gain widespread public support. And if the mass media of communication are gagged, that support is difficult to achieve. Some newspapers did report the packaging hearings objectively in their news columns, and a few supported the Hart bill editorially. But many more derided the purpose of the hearings and characterized the bill as a threat to free enterprise. And while television remained silent, and the mass-circulation magazines concocted hosannas to the food manufacturers, the trade magazines in the food, packaging, and advertising industries attacked the bill viciously. Said *Food Business*: "No nightmare, this is reality. It's the great witch hunt: 1961. What Salem did for its witches in 1692 may yet become a minute affair in comparison to the trial taking shape for the food industry." "If the bill is passed now," said *Printers' Ink*, "it will represent a massive and conscious rejection of the needs of consumers and business." *Modern Packaging* warned that "Washington's current attack on 'deceptive packaging' has created a situation of the utmost seriousness. . . . No thinking person can deny that packaging in general has suffered an unwarranted black eye as a result of the hullabaloo being raised by the Senate investigation." In an article titled "Here's Package You Won't Buy," *Nation's Business* reported that the possibility of packaging legislation was "raising industry fears of requirements that could stifle competition, disrupt mass distribution, and force prices upward." *Pulp & Paper* ran an editorial headed: "That phony Hart Bill is back again—threat to mills, labor, whole economy."

This unanimous hostility in the trade press was understandable. These were, after all, the food, packaging, and advertising people talking to themselves. And perhaps little harm was done. But what about *Life, Look, Reader's Digest,* the *Saturday Evening Post,* and *Ladies' Home Journal?* Shouldn't they be expected to tell the whole story to their readers, the housewives who annually poured $80 billion into the supermarket till?

It is no secret that newspapers, large-circulation magazines, and television networks are big business. And they depend for their existence on the favor of other big business—the bankers for credit, and the advertisers for cash. There was a day, long ago, when journalism in America was dominated by the small, independent, privately owned journal of opinion, supported primarily by faithful and devoted subscribers to the wit, intelligence, and insight of the editor. But the trend from individual to collective enterprise that marked the rise of the great industrial corporations following the Civil War also touched the publishing world, transforming the magazine and the newspaper from vehicles of opinion to profit-making enterprises, complete with boards of directors and stockholders.

By the turn of the century, newspapers and magazines were deriving the bulk of their revenue from advertising. But long before then, the handwriting was on the wall. Writing in *A Practical Treatise on Business,* Edwin Trosall Freedley said, in 1852: "The true merchant will be a liberal but discriminating supporter of the press in his locality. He will combine with men like himself to procure the establishment of such a journal as is needed, or the transfer of one already existing into the hands of someone qualified to guide opinion and dispel mental darkness. Such a journal he will liberally and steadily encourage and support by advertising in its columns at good prices, by urging upon other business men the duty of doing likewise, and by soliciting his customers and neighbors to give it their subscriptions." In this way, the businessman would be able to "exert a noiseless, unintermitted influence in diminishing the kingdom of darkness, extending the range of virtue, and laying deep and broad the foundations of general and personal prosperity."

By the beginning of the twentieth century, this ability to "exert a noiseless, unintermitted influence" was brought to bear on a pernicious problem. There had arisen, in the newspapers and popular magazines, a phenomenon known as "muckraking." This was the name given by Theodore Roosevelt to a type of reporting that pulled no punches in delineating the antisocial practices of politicians and the "robber barons" of big business. Typical of the genre was a series by Ida Tarbell in *McClure's* on the Standard Oil Company. Circulation of the muckraking magazines skyrocketed. Readers ate it up. But Richard Hofstadter, in *The Age of Reform,* tells how this type of journalism died:

"If, from the standpoint of the editors and journalists themselves, the beginning of muckraking seemed to be more or less 'accidental,' its ending did not. The large magazine built on muckraking was vulnerable as a business organization. The publishing firm was so

large an enterprise and sold its product for so little that it became
intensely dependent upon advertising and credit, and hence vulnerable to pressure from the business community. Advertisers did not
hesitate to withdraw orders for space when their own interests or
related interests were touched upon. Bankers adopted a discriminatory credit policy, so that modest loans could not be secured even
for the maintenance of a business of great value and proved
stability. In one case, that of *Hampton's*, even espionage was em-
ployed to destroy the magazine."

Some methods of exerting influence were more subtle than those
of Mr. Willis, some less so. One not-so-subtle method was con-
ceived by F. J. Cheney, peddler of Hall's Catarrh Cure, and
adopted by members of the Proprietary Association, a trade association of the drug industry, to fight passage of the 1906 Pure
Food and Drug Act. Mr. Cheney and his colleagues simply printed
in big red letters, on the advertising contracts with every newspaper
and magazine, a clause stating that the contract would be void if
any legislation hostile to the drug industry were passed. The "red
clause" served as a constant reminder to the publisher which side
his bread was buttered on. A few magazines, like *Collier's* and
Ladies' Home Journal, resisted intimidation, but most knuckled
under.

Strong-arm methods such as these, and naked power plays such
as that of Mr. Willis, are rarely needed today. Since newspaper
and magazine publishing is big business, its interests and those of
industry usually coincide. This is reflected in a tendency for the
press to contribute to the maintenance of the status quo. Or, as
A. J. Liebling put it: "Because of publishers' wealth, they do not
have to be slugged over the head by 'anti-democratic organizations'
to force them into using their properties to form public opinion the
N.A.M. approves. The gesture would be as redundant as twisting a
nymphomaniac's arm to get her into bed."

Mr. Liebling was writing about newspapers, where the situation
is bad enough. In other forms of journalism, according to John
Tebbel, professor of journalism at NYU, the situation "is even more
depressing. Advertisers own the other media, body and soul. Newspapers sometimes print things that offend advertisers, and a few

of them oppose the interests of business, but no mass circulation magazine does so. Only the small and largely subsidized journals of opinion dare to say what they think. Magazines have become more and more an entertainment medium." And, Professor Tebbel might have added, television was never anything else.

The vote of a United States senator or congressman is influenced by his own judgment, the advice of his colleagues, the will of his party leaders, the pressure of lobbyists, and the voice of his constituents. Unless the voice of his constituents is loud and clear, other influences are likely to be overriding. This problem becomes especially acute in areas such as automobile safety, drug efficacy, and packaging and labeling, which promise to benefit the individual consumer while impugning the business practices of a powerful and wealthy industry. The voice of the industry is strong and unequivocal. The voice of the consumer is weak and confused. The weakness and confusion bespeak a lack of hard information on which to base a judgment. As Senator Hart said in May, 1966, "The chief reason the bill has not been enacted thus far . . . is this difference in the power to communicate." Over the five years that marked the struggle to pass a packaging bill, it was probably true, as the agents of the mass media claimed, that the clamor of the general public to their congressmen for passage of the bill was notable by its absence.

For the people had not been told. Although much lip service is paid in this country to the principle of an informed electorate, it seems clear that the electorate depends for its information, to an unhealthy degree, upon those who have a vested interest in influencing their judgments. Unless some means can be found to unclog the channels of mass communication, there is some question whether a popular democracy can survive in a technological age.

14

Business and Government

The five-year struggle to enact a truth-in-packaging bill was a battle launched by government to win new positions behind the lines of business in the interest of the public welfare. The defending generals of the corporations cried "intrusion" and warned of the destruction of the free enterprise system. Their minions of the trade press impugned the motives of the politicians, charging them with currying the favor of the voters in order to feed their already swollen power. This was one more battle in a war that, in a free society, could never end. The battle lines were indistinct, and the rules unclear.

Among the onlookers, for whom the battle was being fought, there were mixed feelings. The words "free enterprise" on the one hand and "monopoly" on the other are charged with emotion, and most of those in the vast middle ground looked with some suspicion on both combatants. Over the battleground there still lingered traces of the old myth that free and untrammeled commercial endeavor works naturally to the best interest of the consumer. The air was also tinged with echoes from bruising battles of half a century and more ago, in which the powers of the gluttonous "trusts" were curbed. Where was the right?

One thing was clear from the record: some results of commercial enterprise were plainly antisocial. Fraudulent and misleading labeling and advertising; useless or harmful drugs; adulteration of foods;

discriminatory pricing for favored customers; exploitation of labor; corruption of the earth's bounty (water and air pollution, depletion of resources, dirt, odors, blight); rigging of the securities market; "administered" prices; and collusion to fix prices and allocate shares of the market—all these ills had come under public scrutiny, and some had been dosed by legislation. None of them had been cured naturally by the free play of forces in a free market, in accordance with the ancient and now discredited ethic of the marketplace.

But those who, outraged by these ills, call the corporation evil or castigate the corporation manager as irresponsible misunderstand the proper roles of the corporation and its manager in our society. The reason for the existence of a corporation is to make money. Profit is its most important product. In the process of making a profit, it does a number of socially desirable things: it creates jobs; it makes available to the public useful gadgets that ease the day-by-day routine maintenance of life; and, if it is an "enlightened" corporation, it diverts a trickle of the gold flow into good works such as scholarships, hospitals, community chests, and so on. But the men who build the corporation do so not to create jobs for deserving workers, not to provide their fellow men with labor-saving devices, not to furnish investors an opportunity to multiply their capital, but to make money.

The good corporate manager keeps his eye on this ball. He feels keenly his responsibility to his stockholders, his employees, his customers, and the community in which he lives. But unless the corporation makes a profit, it and all its good works will disappear. He would like to pay a dividend to his stockholders, but if he can persuade them to feed the money back into the business, he will. He does provide good jobs for thousands of people, but if he can do it better with machines, he will. He knows that a satisfied customer is his *sine qua non,* but whether his product satisfies a real or an imagined want is a matter of indifference to him. Good works in the community may gratify him personally, but they are most readily justified to his board of directors on the basis of improving the image of the corporation.

Is all this wrong? It most assuredly is not. The profit motive is the most efficient fuel ever discovered for making the industrial machinery run. The difficulty arises from the fact that we have come to expect more from the corporation than it can, by its nature, deliver. And the corporation encourages us in this misplaced trust. Uncomfortable in its role as a money-maker, it wishes us to believe that it is a public-spirited citizen, put here on earth to provide jobs and to make the blessings of technology available to society. A veritable army of public relations writers grind out this propaganda daily by the ton.

The individual who suffers most from this confusion of values is the corporation manager himself. On the one hand, he understands clearly the mandate from his board of directors: "Do whatever is necessary, within the law, to increase profit." On the other hand, he must deal with a public that is awash in his own propaganda. In the words of Arthur Selwin Miller, he is "groping in an ethical wilderness." When a conflict arises between the corporate welfare and the public welfare, we hope that he will act the statesman. Half believing his own propaganda, he may wish that he could, but he knows that he cannot. What is good for General Motors may or may not be good for the country, but when the chips are down his choice is clear.

Once we grant to the corporate manager that which is his—a single-minded devotion to profit, with no stigma attached—and once we perceive that the untrammeled drive to profit can as easily result in a social ill as a social good, it becomes clear that a referee is needed to make the ethical decision. This is the role of government.

It is in the nature of the corporate manager to resist intrusion by government. When an abuse is brought to light, his first reaction is to deny its existence. This failing, he then suggests that the best solution is self-regulation by industry. This can be done, he says, by a trade association or by a special council of industry representatives, who will study the problem and devise a code of ethics for all to subscribe to. Such efforts are doomed to failure. As long as regulation remains voluntary, there is always the dissenter who is willing to gain a competitive advantage by ignoring the code. And the code is likely to be innocuous in the first place. Typical is the code devised in 1963 by the Packaging Institute to take the steam out of the Hart bill. Even *Modern Packaging* magazine, hardly an advocate of the bill, wrote that the institute had "labored and brought forth a mouse."

Charles G. Mortimer of General Foods typified the attitude of the corporate manager toward government "intervention" in a statement quoted in *Food & Drug Packaging* magazine: "I am increasingly concerned as I witness the growing addiction to paternalism which is taking such a firm hold on this nation. As more and more monolithic structures have sprung up along the banks of the Potomac, government has assayed [sic] the role of omnipotent doer of good and solver of problems—the sole guardian of the public interest. This has been brought home most forcefully in recent months as word has come from Washington of the government's newest 'discovery'—the consumer. Increasingly, there are strong suggestions from our nation's capital that . . . the federal government is the only element in this democracy qualified or interested enough to try to improve her lot."

It is plain that the government *is* "the sole guardian of the public interest." The role of General Foods Corporation in our society is to make money selling groceries. The role of government is to see that General Foods, in fulfilling its role, uses methods that neither harm the consumer nor degrade the competitive vigor of the marketplace. General Foods would have us believe that it is interested in improving the lot of the housewife. It is true, of course, that competition in the grocery business often results in food products of higher quality and greater convenience. But it is also true that competition often results in products that deceive and betray the housewife. And General Foods, in its rightful and single-minded pursuit of profit, is not as sensitive to the difference as we might wish.

The monolithic structures along the Potomac have sprung up to act as a counterweight in a society that is dominated by gigantic centers of corporate power. General Foods enjoys annual sales of nearly $1.5 billion—greater than the total revenues for the state of Pennsylvania. General Motors, the king of them all, happily receives each year for sales of its products an amount greater than the combined revenue for the states of Alabama, Alaska, Arizona, Arkansas, California, Colorado, Connecticut, Delaware, Florida, Georgia, Hawaii, Idaho, Illinois, Indiana, Iowa, Kansas, Kentucky, Louisiana, Maine, Maryland, Massachusetts, Michigan, Minnesota, Mississippi, Missouri, Montana, Nebraska, Nevada, and New Hampshire. As large as those buildings in Washington may appear to a citizenry tutored to abhor bureaucracy, there is still some question whether the balance has yet been redressed.

15

The Packaging Law

The first hearings to determine whether packaging legislation was needed were held by the Antitrust and Monopoly Subcommittee of the Senate Judiciary Committee during June, October, and December of 1961 and February, March, and April of 1962. At these hearings, 41 witnesses testified and 22 statements were placed in the record. On January 21, 1963, Senator Hart introduced his truth-in-packaging bill in the Senate. Hearings on the bill were held during March and April, 1963, during which 47 witnesses were heard and 46 statements were submitted. On June 13, the bill was reported favorably to the Judiciary Committee. During the remainder of 1963 and the whole of 1964, the Judiciary Committee took no action, and the bill died with the close of the 88th Congress in 1964.

Senator Hart re-introduced the bill in 1965 to the 89th Congress and had it moved from the Senate Judiciary Committee to the Commerce Committee. No action was taken in 1965. On May 13, 1966, the bill was finally reported out of the Commerce Committee. It passed the Senate on June 9 by a vote of 72 to 9, in a somewhat weakened state. The House Commerce Committee then held hearings in July, August, and September, 1966, during which 99 witnesses were heard and 145 statements and exhibits were placed in the record. The committee then killed the Senate bill and proceeded to write a bill of its own, which resembled the original Hart bill only in name. This substitute bill passed the House on October 3, 1966, by a lopsided 300–8 vote. The Senate accepted the House "revision," and on November 3 President Johnson signed it. On that day, the bill became Public Law 89-755, the "Fair Packaging and Labeling Act," with an effective date of July 1, 1967.

Some observers, after reading PL 89-755, commented that it appeared to be a joint effort of the congressmen and the food lobbyists. One strong supporter of the bill said that "industry's fingerprints are all over it." A Herblock cartoon published the day after the House vote shows an irate consumer shaking a box of dry cereal bearing the legend "New Congressional House Size Super Shredded Truth-in-Packaging Bill, Fortified with Genuine Hot Air." Four lonesome shredded flakes are falling out of the box. The consumer is saying to a sheepish congressman: "This is supposed to serve 200,000,000?"

The House bill, said the *New York Times,* was "little more than a shadow" of the original bill. During the brief debate on the House floor, said the *Times,* most of the protest had come from supporters of stronger legislation. They said they would vote for the bill, but they considered it inadequate. "My complaint," said Congresswoman Leonor K. Sullivan, "is that it does so little." Despite the widespread dissatisfaction, however, the vote was overwhelmingly in favor of passage; the word had come down from the committee that it was this bill or nothing.

Columnists who read the bill agreed that the House version was a mere shadow of the original Hart bill. Marquis Childs wrote: "The kernel of truth left in the truth-in-packaging bill after it came through the wringer of the House Commerce Committee is so tiny that the backers of the measure have seriously thought that it might be better to let it go down to defeat and start afresh in the new Congress." The food lobbyists, said Mr. Childs, had won a notable victory. "Generalissimo of these forces," was George A. Koch, successor to Paul S. Willis as president of Grocery Manufacturers of America. According to Mr. Childs, members of the House Commerce Committee had heard Mr. Koch boast that he would gut the bill singlehanded. One copy of the House version of the bill had contained what was labeled the "Koch amendment to permit innovations in the packaging of consumer commodities."

"A first report by the House Commerce Committee," wrote columnist I. F. Stone, which had been "quickly withdrawn," revealed that the House version of the bill had been written with the help of the "affected industries." "In order to get the bill to the House floor at all, its supporters had to pledge ('our souls,' as one of them put it)" that they would allow no revisions of the bill on the floor. Whether or not the affected industries had a hand in writing the bill, said Senator Hart, "I know they were happy with the treatment of package standardization."

The man who deserved the credit for emasculating the bill, according to Drew Pearson, was "William Murphy, head of Campbell Soup. Murphy is chairman of the Business Council, which is the President's business advisory group. He is close to the White House, especially to Mr. Johnson's shrewd adviser, Joe Califano. Murphy sweet-talked the powers that be into yanking the heart of the packaging standards out of the White House bill." Supporting him were a number of members of the House Commerce Committee with large food industries in their districts.

Senator Warren G. Magnuson of Washington, chairman of the Senate Commerce Committee, said that, in the House-Senate conference which finally accepted the House version, the conference committee members from the House were adamant. "The choice confronting us was to accept [the House] version or to have no bill at all." The final bill, he said, was "not a truth-in-packaging bill. Rather, it is essentially a labeling bill."

The packaging act, Public Law 89-755, has provisions relating to the placement and size of the net contents on the label, and it restricts the use of "jumbo" adjectives. Neither of these labeling matters had been strongly contested by industry. It provides for regulations to prohibit the use of "nonfunctional" slack fill in packages. But the long, tortuous history of the Delson Thin Mint case offers little hope that the word "nonfunctional" is definitive.

The Hart bill would have prohibited cents-off announcements on the package. The law merely gives the FDA and the FTC discretionary power to "regulate" cents-off labels "if necessary to prevent the deception of consumers." Presumably this gives the

FDA and the FTC police power to ensure that the cents-off label is honest; that is, that the consumer truly experiences the saving promised by the label. This is an impossible assignment. As Senator Hart put it during the 1965 hearings: "Inasmuch as there are approximately 274,000 retail outlets for food products in this country, and literally hundreds of cents-off deals and economy size designations in each, an army of investigators would be needed to police only this kind of practice. Certainly, the spectacle of an army of Government investigators moving into the markets to enforce the promise of a manufacturer which he can't control himself is not the answer to this problem."

The Hart bill would have given the FDA the power to establish a standard definition for a "serving" of a given food, so that the word "serving" would mean the same for all brands of the same food. The law merely gives the FDA the power to require that a manufacturer who specifies servings show on his label what his own private definition of a serving is. The consumer, then, will have to decide among three servings at 3⅛ ounces each, four servings at 2⅜ ounces each, and five servings at 1⅞ ounces each.

The Hart bill would have prohibited the placement of deceptive illustrations on the package. There is no such provision in the law.

The Hart bill provided for regulations to prevent the distribution of commodities "in packages of sizes, shapes, or dimensional proportions which are likely to deceive retail purchasers in any material respect as to the net quantity of the contents." There is no such provision in the law.

Finally, the essence of the Hart bill lay in its provisions for simplifying the weights and measures of net contents of packages to enable the shopper to determine the price per ounce or per pound and to eliminate the insidious shell game of packaging to price. This is where truth in packaging must stand or fall, and this is where the Hart bill was emasculated. The Hart bill gave the FDA and FTC discretionary power to issue regulations to "establish reasonable weights or quantities, or fractions or multiples thereof, in which [a] commodity shall be distributed for retail sale." The paragraph of Section 5 of PL 89-755 purporting to deal with this major problem are worth quoting:

(d). Whenever the Secretary of Commerce determines that there is undue proliferation of the weights, measures, or quantities in which any consumer commodity or reasonably comparable consumer commodities are being distributed in packages for sale at retail and such undue proliferation impairs the reasonable ability of consumers to make value comparisons with respect to such consumer commodity or commodities, he shall request manufacturers, packers, and distributors of the commodity or commodities to participate in the development of a voluntary product standard for such commodity or commodities under the procedures for the development of voluntary products standards established by the Secretary pursuant to Section 2 of the Act of March 3, 1901 (31 Stat. 1449, as amended: 15 U.S.C. 272). Such procedures shall provide adequate manufacturer, packer, distributor, and consumer representation.

(e) If (1) after one year after the date on which the Secretary of Commerce first makes the request of manufacturers, packers, and distributors to participate in the development of a voluntary product standard as provided in subsection (d) of this section, he determines that such a standard will not be published pursuant to the provisions of such subsection (d), or (2) if such a standard is published and the Secretary of Commerce determines that it has not been observed, he shall promptly report such determination to the Congress with a statement of the efforts that have been made under the voluntary standards program and his recommendation as to whether Congress should enact legislation providing regulatory authority to deal with the situation in question.

Whereas the Hart bill gave the FDA and the FTC authority to regulate the net contents of packages, the law asks the Secretary of Commerce to persuade industry groups, with the help of consumers, to write "voluntary" standards. If persuasion fails, the Secretary may go to Congress and ask for additional legislation.

In his analysis of the final legislation, Senator Hart called it "strong," but it was clear he had in mind chiefly the hope that, by passing *any* packaging bill, Congress had indicated an interest in this type of consumer legislation.

He saw this bill as the thin end of a wedge. Several weeks after its passage into law, Senator Hart said, "When you look at that bill, and you say it took five years—my God, that's a long time, and it is—but some of those things in that bill had been kicking around Congress for that long individually. . . . But, to get it

on the books! To get a toehold is worth a session of Congress. . . .
I think the way package standardization was treated in my original
bill was good—that was strong. This bill doesn't approach that.
When I speak of this being a strong bill, I am contrasting it to
what we were threatened with. I think that the bill originally, on
standardization, was far more effective. But we couldn't get it."

The responsibility for package standardization was taken from
the Food and Drug Administration and the Federal Trade Commission and given to the Department of Commerce. Whereas the FDA
and the FTC are traditionally consumer-oriented agencies, the
Department of Commerce is a business-oriented agency. The
mission of the FDA is to protect the general welfare by barring
from the market any harmful foods and harmful or ineffective
drugs. The FTC exists to protect the consumer from the effects of
unfair competition, deceptive practices, false advertising, price
discrimination, and monopolies. The mission of the Department of
Commerce, on the other hand, is to foster, promote, and develop
the nation's commerce. The agencies within the department were
created to assist the businessman: Business and Defense Services
Administration, Office of Business Economics, Patent Office,
Bureau of the Census, Coast and Geodetic Survey, Weather
Bureau (now Environmental Science Services), Bureau of Standards, Bureau of International Commerce, Maritime Administration, Bureau of Public Roads.

The reluctance of the Commerce Department to become involved in consumer legislation has been noted before. Ralph
Nader, crusader for automobile safety, commented that, in view of
its business orientation, the department was "unsuited to handle
consumer protection laws. The consumer's interest would take
second place to the interests of the business community. This is
the reason why manufacturing interests always try to steer what
consumer legislation they cannot defeat over to the Commerce
Department."

Asked for his views on this, Senator Hart agreed: "Sure, the role
of the Department of Commerce is to promote American business.
So it doesn't have the responsibility or the traditions that the Department of Justice, in the Antitrust Division, the Food and Drug

Administration, or the Federal Trade Commission have. Against that tradition and background and purpose, it is understandable that consumer legislation would get a different treatment in Commerce."

Under the provisions of the packaging law, nothing will happen to correct any abuse in the major areas of fractionalized weights or packaging to price until the Secretary of Commerce believes there is abuse. There is some question whether the Secretary of Commerce, a business-oriented head of a department formed to promote the welfare of business, is the man for the job.

Since President Kennedy and President Johnson paid at least lip service to truth-in-packaging legislation, their Secretaries of Commerce—Luther H. Hodges and John T. Connor—testified in favor of the Hart bill. But their support was somewhat less than zealous. As Senator Hart said later, "There were times when we wondered how long Commerce would stay with us under the attack the bill was getting."

In March, 1963, Secretary Hodges told the Hart subcommittee that "my basic preference is for as little Government regulation as possible. I think individuals and industries should set their own high standards of conduct and follow these standards. . . . While *our special concern for this bill relates to the interest of the Department of Commerce in the business community,* I certainly do not overlook the importance of this legislation to the consumer [italics added]."

A little later, Secretary Hodges emphasized this point: "I have said to my business friends all over the country that I wish we did not have a single regulatory agency. I wish it had been possible that the public had had its protection fully so that none would have ever been created, and I would say the same thing to any other industry that might have to have regulation."

Secretary Hodges was reluctant to believe that any new packaging legislation was necessary: "I think the questions raised a while ago [relative to the adequacy of existing law] are certainly good and searching questions, and I gather that . . . there is a difference of opinion as to whether or not we now have adequate laws and regulations. I would not have an opinion on that. I would certainly say this: That if, in the judgment of yourselves and your staff, working with these agencies, you find they have the laws and the personnel, I would certainly hate to add either to the law or to the personnel."

In April, 1965, newly appointed Commerce Secretary John Connor testified in defense of his business friends: "I should like to express clearly my opinion that the vast majority of business firms responsible for packaging and labeling of our products do not engage in deceptive or questionable practices but rather adhere to highly commendable standards of merchandising. Nevertheless, there are some abuses in this area by a small minority and I believe that the previous hearings have shown that there is a need for some improvements in our existing laws."

If Secretary Connor truly believed that the vast majority of food manufacturers and packagers have not engaged in deceptive or questionable practices, he had not read the record. In his testimony to the House Commerce Committee in July, 1966, he came out strongly for "self-regulation" by industry, through the "voluntary" standardization procedures of the Department of Commerce: "As I stated in my testimony last year before the Senate Commerce Committee, the Department of Commerce is hopeful that appropriate use would be made of its voluntary product standards program. . . . If a voluntary standard on weights and quantities is published within the time prescribed [in the Senate bill], any regulations which are promulgated by the enforcing agencies, FTC and FDA, could not vary from the existing standard. Indeed, if there is compliance with the voluntary standard, there may be no need for regulation. In a very real sense, this is a form of self-regulation." The House went the extra mile with Secretary Connor by eliminating the FDA and the FTC from the picture entirely.

The voluntary standardization program of the Commerce Department is truly voluntary in every sense of the word. The government may invite industry to prepare a standard, and industry may comply or not, as it sees fit. Further, once a standard is written, industry may use it or not, as it wishes. A review of the industry testimony at the packaging hearings gives rise to some doubt that the voluntary cooperation of industry will be forthcoming in any standardization effort.

At a conference in Washington on February 28, 1967, four months after enactment of the packaging law, Robert E. Giles, general counsel for the Department of Commerce, told several hundred businessmen in the food and packaging industries that his Department was not going to cause any discomfort among them by issuing regulations. The Commerce Department, he said, is involved only with "the portion of this law dealing with the development of voluntary product standards.

"The word 'voluntary,' unlike the word 'regulation,' is usually regarded as a nice word," he went on. "I would even go so far as to say that voluntary is a happy word. It has a connotation of happy things being done by happy people—not unhappy things being done *to* unhappy people." An appreciative ripple of happy laughter swept through his audience.

Business Week magazine wrote that Secretary Connor "conceives his role as that of Businessman's Representative in the Johnson Administration," and that his interest is in government policies to "encourage and nourish the growth and success of private business." This should come as no surprise, since this is understood to be the role of the Secretary of Commerce. In his recommendation to the House Commerce Committee for voluntary standards, Secretary Connor played a key role in the gutting of the Hart bill.

In her syndicated column of November 20, 1966, Marianne Means wrote that many of Secretary Connor's fellow officials had come to regard him as merely "an apologist for industry" who was uncomfortable in the role of protector of the consumer which was being thrust upon him. "Frequently he has privately opposed the very programs he has been expected to sponsor on Capitol Hill," she wrote. "He secretly encouraged industry opposition to the truth-in-packaging bill, for instance, and dragged his heels when assigned the responsibility for pushing it through Congress." Two months after this column appeared, Connor had resigned. His successor is Alexander B. Trowbridge, formerly president and division manager of Esso Standard Oil Company of Puerto Rico.

Although not optimistic about the role of the Secretary of Commerce in enforcing the packaging law, Senator Hart is not without hope. "A fellow who is Secretary of Commerce," he remarked, "is uneasy at being portrayed to business and industry, whose voice he is in the Cabinet, as the voice of the consumer. That's understandable. But it doesn't mean that he can't go to them and say, 'Look, by God, the Congress says to put those labels on this way!' "

Further, some say, President Johnson wanted truth in packaging, and he has told the Secretary of Commerce publicly to get cracking and enforce the new law. The President, however, although periodically espousing packaging legislation in his public utterances, never publicly endorsed the Hart bill. "All Johnson wanted," a member of the House Commerce Committee said, "was a bill he could call a 'Truth-in-Packaging' Act. He didn't care what was in it."

For the sake of argument, however, let us assume that, despite his business orientation, the Secretary of Commerce attempts to carry out his responsibilities to the consumer under the packaging law. Having found an abusive packaging situation in, say, detergents, he must call together the manufacturers, packers, and distributors of detergents and ask them to produce a set of standards regulating the weights and sizes of detergent packages, by procedures in which the consumer will have "adequate" representation. He must then give the industry one year to comply. During this year, of course, the abuse continues. Then comes the *coup de grâce*. If, at the end of the year, the Secretary finds that no standard, or an ineffective standard, has been published, he must return to Congress with a recommendation for new legislation to correct the abuse.

Is it likely that Congress would then enact legislation?

The answer to this question is contained in the comments of S. Jerry Cohen on the day the packaging bill finally went to the floor of the House for a vote. Chief counsel and staff director for the Senate Subcommittee on Antitrust and Monopoly at that time, Mr. Cohen, though a youthful-looking forty-one, was six years older than on the day the first packaging hearing opened,

June 28, 1961. Puffing slowly on a cigar, he told an interviewer that the moment of truth had arrived.

"If we don't pass the bill this time, we're dead," he said. "Just now we have the right combination of circumstances, and we'll never have them again. The consumer is aroused, the bill has passed the Senate, we're getting very near adjournment, it's an election year, and the President wants this bill. It's on the top of his 'must' pile."

Mr. Cohen slouched in his chair and stared quietly at the opposite wall. The sound of a million words of argument from five years of testimony echoed through his mind. At that moment, the House of Representatives was voting to pass its packaging bill by an overwhelming majority. The Hart bill was dead.

89TH CONGRESS
1ST SESSION

S. 985

A BILL

To regulate interstate and foreign commerce by preventing the use of unfair or deceptive methods of packaging or labeling of certain consumer commodities distributed in such commerce, and for other purposes.

By Mr. HART, Mr. BARTLETT, Mr. CLARK, Mr. DOUGLAS, Mr. KENNEDY of New York, Mr. LONG of Missouri, Mr. MCINTYRE, Mr. MCNAMARA, Mr. METCALF, Mr. MONDALE, Mr. MUSKIE, Mrs. NEUBERGER, and Mr. RIBICOFF

FEBRUARY 3, 1965

Read twice and referred to the Committee on Commerce

S. 985

IN THE SENATE OF THE UNITED STATES

FEBRUARY 3, 1965

Mr. HART (for himself, Mr. BARTLETT, Mr. CLARK, Mr. DOUGLAS, Mr. KENNEDY of New York, Mr. LONG of Missouri, Mr. MCINTYRE, Mr. MCNAMARA, Mr. METCALF, Mr. MONDALE, Mr. MUSKIE, Mrs. NEUBERGER, and Mr. RIBICOFF) introduced the following bill; which was read twice and referred to the Committee on Commerce

A BILL

To regulate interstate and foreign commerce by preventing the use of unfair or deceptive methods of packaging or labeling of certain consumer commodities distributed in such commerce, and for other purposes.

1 *Be it enacted by the Senate and House of Representa-*

2 *tives of the United States of America in Congress assembled,*

3 That this Act may be cited as the "Fair Packaging and

4 Labeling Act".

5 PROHIBITION OF UNFAIR AND DECEPTIVE PACKAGING AND

6 LABELING

7 SEC. 2. (a) It shall be unlawful for any person engaged

8 in the packaging or labeling of any consumer commodity

VII—O

1   (as defined by this Act) for distribution in commerce, or

2   for any person (other than a common carrier for hire, a

3   contract carrier for hire, or a freight forwarder for hire)

4   engaged in the distribution in commerce of any packaged or

5   labeled consumer commodity, to distribute or to cause to be

6   distributed in commerce any such commodity if such com-

7   modity is contained in a package, or if there is affixed to that

8   commodity a label, which does not conform to regulations

9   promulgated pursuant to this Act.

10   (b) The prohibition contained in subsection (a) shall

11   not apply to persons engaged in business as wholesale or

12   retail distributors of consumer commodities except to the

13   extent that such persons (1) are engaged in the packaging

14   or labeling of such commodities, or (2) prescribe or specify

15   by any means the manner in which such commodities are

16   packaged or labeled.

17   REGULATIONS TO BE PROMULGATED

18   SEC. 3. (a) As soon as practicable after the effective

19   date of this Act, regulations shall be promulgated to—

20   (1) require the net quantity of contents (in terms

21   of weight, measure, or count, or any combination there-

22   of) of consumer commodities to be stated upon the front

23   panel of packages containing such commodities, and upon

24   any labels affixed to such commodities;

25   (2) establish minimum standards with respect to

1   the prominence of statements of the net quantity of con-

2   tents (including minimum standards as to the type size

3   and face in which such statements shall be made) ap-

4   pearing upon packages containing any consumer com-

5   modity and upon labels affixed to any such commodity;

6   (3) prohibit the addition to such statements of net

7   quantity of contents of any qualifying words or phrases;

8   (4) specify such exceptions to the foregoing require-

9   ments as the promulgating authority may determine to be

10   required by the nature, form, or quantity of particular

11   consumer commodities, or by the customary mode of

12   display of any particular consumer commodity for retail

13   sale, except that no exception may be made if that ex-

14   ception would deprive consumers of reasonable oppor-

15   tunity to make rational comparisons between or among

16   competing products;

17   (5) prohibit the placement upon any package con-

18   taining such commodity, or upon any label affixed to

19   such commodity, of any printed matter stating or repre-

20   senting by implication that such commodity is offered

21   for retail sale at a price lower than the ordinary and

22   customary retail sale price, or that a retail sale price

23   advantage is accorded to retail purchasers thereof by

24   reason of the size of that package or the quantity of its

25   contents, except that no regulation promulgated under

1   this section shall prevent any person while engaged at
2   any time in the sale of any consumer commodity at
3   retail to ultimate purchasers thereof from placing upon
4   any such commodity, or upon any package containing
5   that commodity, any marking pertaining to the retail
6   sale price of that commodity; and

7   (6) prevent the placement, upon any package in
8   which such commodity is distributed for retail sale, of
9   any illustration or pictorial matter which is likely to
10 deceive retail purchasers in any material respect as to
11 the contents of that package.

12 (b) (1) Regulations under this section shall be promul-
13 gated by—

14   (A) the Secretary of Health, Education, and Wel-
15 fare (referred to hereinafter as the "Secretary"), with
16 respect to any consumer commodity which is a food,
17 drug, device, or cosmetic, as each such term is defined
18 by section 201 of the Federal Food, Drug, and Cosmetic
19 Act (21 U.S.C. 321) ; and

20   (B) the Federal Trade Commission (referred to
21 hereinafter as the "Commission") with respect to any
22 other consumer commodity.

23 (2) Such regulations adopted by the Secretary and by
24 the Commission shall be uniform in content and application

1 to the greatest practicable extent, as determined by consul-
2 tation between the Secretary and the Commission.

3 (c) Whenever the Secretary (as to any food, drug,
4 device, or cosmetic), or the Commission (as to any other
5 consumer commodity) determines that additional regulations
6 are necessary to establish or preserve fair competition be-
7 tween or among competing products by enabling consumers
8 to make rational comparison with respect to price and other
9 factors, or to prevent the deception of consumers as to such
10 product, the Secretary or the Commission, as the case may
11 be, shall promulgate under this subsection with respect to that
12 commodity regulations effective to—

13   (1) establish reasonable weights or quantities, or
14   fractions or multiples thereof, in which that commodity
15   shall be distributed for retail sale, except that no such
16   regulation may be inconsistent with standards prescribed
17   by the Secretary of Commerce before the effective date
18   of this Act with regard to the sizes of containers used
19   for the retail sale of any commodity, and no weights
20   and measures shall be established in amounts of less
21   than two ounces;

22   (2) prevent the distribution of that commodity for
23   retail sale in packages of sizes, shapes, or dimensional

1   proportions which are likely to deceive retail purchasers
2   in any material respect as to the net quantity of the
3   contents thereof (in terms of weight, measure, or
4   count), except that where reasonable weights and
5   measures have been established pursuant to the provi-
6   sions of paragraph (1) of this subsection such regula-
7   tions may not proscribe the use of package shapes which
8   have been designed to exploit the unique advantages of
9   any material for use in the production of packages of
10   distinctive appearance;

11   (3) establish and define standards of designations of
12   size (other than statements of net quantity of contents)
13   which may be used to characterize quantitatively the
14   contents of packages containing that commodity;

15   (4) establish and define the net quantity of any
16   commodity (in terms of weight, measure, or count)
17   which shall constitute a serving, if that commodity is
18   distributed to retail purchasers in a package or with a
19   label which bears a representation as to the number of
20   servings provided by the net quantity of contents con-
21   tained in that package or to which that label is affixed;

22   (5) establish and define standards for the quantita-
23   tive designation of the contents of packages containing
24   any consumer commodity of a kind the net quantity of

1   contents of which cannot meaningfully be designated in

2   terms of weight, measure, or count; and

3   (6) require (consistent with requirements imposed

4   by or pursuant to the Federal Food, Drug, and Cosmetic

5   Act, as amended) that sufficient information with respect

6   to the ingredients and composition of any consumer com-

7   modity (other than information concerning proprietary

8   trade secrets) be placed in a prominent position upon

9   packages containing that commodity and upon labels

10   affixed thereto.

11   PROCEDURE FOR PROMULGATION OF REGULATIONS

12   SEC. 4. (a) Before promulgating any proposed regula-

13   tion under section 3 with respect to any consumer commodity,

14   the Secretary or the Commission, as the case may be, shall

15   (1) consult with other agencies of the Government having

16   special competence with respect to the subject of that regu-

17   lation concerning the scope, application, form, and effect

18   thereof, (2) publish in the Federal Register reasonable ad-

19   vance notice of intention to promulgate such regulation, and

20   (3) accord to persons who would be affected thereby rea-

21   sonable opportunity for consultation with respect to such

22   proposed regulation.

23   (b) All regulations adopted under this Act shall be

24   promulgated in conformity with the provisions of the Ad-

ministrative Procedure Act. No regulation shall be promulgated for any purpose described in section 3 (c) of this Act unless a public hearing has been conducted and opportunity for review has been accorded in conformity with the provisions of sections 7 and 8 of the Administrative Procedure Act.

(c) Any regulation promulgated under this Act may be modified by the promulgating authority, upon the initiative of that authority or upon application made by any person affected by that regulation, whenever such authority determines that such modification is necessary to conform to the requirements of this Act or to any change occurring in the method of packaging, labeling, distributing, or marketing of any consumer commodity.

(d) No regulation adopted under this Act shall take effect until a reasonable period of time (as determined by the Secretary or the Commission, as the case may be) has passed after the promulgation thereof to permit persons affected thereby to effectuate compliance with the provisions of such regulation.

(e) In carrying into effect the provisions of this Act, the Secretary and the Commission are authorized to cooperate with any department or agency of the United States, with any State, Commonwealth, or possession of the United

1 States, and with any department, agency, or political subdi-
2 vision of any such State, Commonwealth, or possession.

4   SEC. 5. (a) Upon written request made, by the officer
5 or agency authorized or directed by this Act to establish
6 packaging or labeling regulations as to any consumer com-
7 modity of any class or kind, to any producer or distributor
8 of such consumer commodity, such producer or distributor
9 shall transmit promptly to that officer or agency a true
10 and correct sample of each package and label used by that
11 producer or distributor for or in connection with the dis-
12 tribution in commerce of any particularly described consumer
13 commodity of that class or kind. Any person who fails to
14 transmit any such sample to such authority within twenty
15 days after receipt of such request shall be subject to a civil
16 penalty of not more than $1,000 for each day of the con-
17 tinuance of such failure, except that the amount of such
18 penalty may be compromised by such authority before the
19 final determination of action for the recovery thereof. Such
20 forfeiture shall be recovered in a civil action brought in the
21 name of the United States in the district court of the United
22 States for any judicial district in which such person resides,
23 does business, or is found. Upon demand made by the de-
24 fendant before the trial of any such action upon its merits,

1 the defendant shall be entitled to have any issue of fact
2 with respect to such failure determined by a jury.

3   (b) Any consumer commodity introduced or delivered
4 for introduction into commerce in violation of any regulation
5 promulgated by the Secretary of Health, Education, and
6 Welfare under this Act while that regulation is in force and
7 in effect shall be deemed to be misbranded within the
8 meaning of chapter III of the Federal Food, Drug, and
9 Cosmetic Act, but the provisions of section 303 of that
10 Act (21 U.S.C. 333) shall have no application to any
11 violation of any such regulation.

12   (c) Any violation of any regulation promulgated under
13 this Act by the Federal Trade Commission while that regula-
14 tion is in force and in effect shall constitute an unfair or
15 deceptive act or practice in commerce in violation of section
16 5 (a) of the Federal Trade Commission Act. The remedies
17 provided by sections 4, 4A, and 16 of the Act entitled "An
18 Act to supplement existing laws against unlawful restraints
19 and monopolies, and for other purposes", approved October
20 15, 1914 (38 Stat. 730, as amended; 15 U.S.C. 15, 15a, and
21 26), commonly known as the Clayton Act, shall not be
22 available to any person threatened with loss or damage, or
23 injured in his business or property, by any violation of any
24 such regulation under this Act.

2 SEC. 6. Each officer or agency required or authorized
3 by this section to promulgate regulations for the packaging
4 or labeling of any consumer commodity shall transmit to the
5 Congress in January of each year a report containing a full
6 and complete description of the activities of that officer or
7 agency for the administration and enforcement of this Act
8 during the preceding calendar year.

9 COOPERATION WITH STATE AUTHORITIES

10 SEC. 7. (a) A copy of each regulation promulgated
11 under this Act shall be transmitted promptly to the Secre-
12 tary of Commerce, who shall (1) transmit copies thereof
13 to all appropriate State officers and agencies, and (2) furnish
14 to such State officers and agencies information and assistance
15 to promote to the greatest practicable extent uniformity in
16 State and Federal standards for the packaging and labeling of
17 consumer commodities.

18 (b) Nothing contained in this section shall be construed
19 to impair or otherwise interfere with any program carried
20 into effect by the Secretary of Health, Education, and Wel-
21 fare under other provisions of law in cooperation with State
22 governments or agencies, instrumentalities, or political sub-
23 divisions thereof.

SEC. 8. As used in this section—

(1) The term "commerce" has the meaning given thereto by section 4 of the Federal Trade Commission Act (15 U.S.C. 44).

(2) The term "consumer commodity", except as otherwise specifically provided by this paragraph, means any food, drug, device, or cosmetic (as those terms are defined by the Federal Food, Drug, and Cosmetic Act), and any other article or commodity of any kind or class which is customarily produced or distributed for sale through retail sales agencies or instrumentalities for consumption by individuals, or use by individuals for purposes of personal care or in the performance of services ordinarily rendered within the household, and which usually is consumed or expended in the course of such consumption or use. Such term does not include (A) any meat, meat product, poultry, or poultry product, (B) any commodity subject to packaging or labeling requirements imposed by the Secretary of Agriculture pursuant to the Federal Insecticide, Fungicide, and Rodenticide Act, the provisions of the eighth paragraph under the heading "Bureau of Animal Industry" of the Act of March 4, 1913 (37 Stat. 832–833; 21 U.S.C. 151–157), commonly known as the Virus-Serum-Toxin

1   Act; (C) any beverage subject to or complying with
2   packaging or labeling requirements imposed under the
3   Federal Alcohol Administration Act (27 U.S.C. 201
4   et seq.) ; or (D) any commodity subject to the pro-
5   visions of the Federal Seed Act (7 U.S.C. 1551–1610).

6   (3) The term "package" means any container or
7   wrapping in which any consumer commodity is enclosed
8   for use in the delivery or display of that commodity to
9   retail purchasers thereof, but does not include (A)
10   shipping containers or wrappings used solely for the
11   transportation of such commodity in bulk or in quantity
12   to wholesale or retail distributors thereof, (B) shipping
13   containers or outer wrappings used by retailers to ship
14   or deliver such commodity to retail customers if such
15   containers and wrappings bear no printed matter per-
16   taining to any particular commodity, or (C) containers
17   subject to the provisions of the Act of August 3, 1912
18   (37 Stat. 250, as amended; 15 U.S.C. 231–233), the
19   Act of March 4, 1915 (38 Stat. 1186, as amended;
20   15 U.S.C. 234–236), the Act of August 31, 1916 (39
21   Stat. 673, as amended; 15 U.S.C. 251–256), or the
22   Act of May 21, 1928 (45 Stat. 685, as amended; 15
23   U.S.C. 257–257i).

24   (4) The term "label" means any written, printed,
25   or graphic matter affixed to any consumer commodity.

1   (5) The term "person" includes any firm, corpora-
2 tion, or association.

3

4 SEC. 9. Nothing contained in this Act shall be construed
5 to repeal, invalidate, supersede, or otherwise adversely
6 affect—

7   (a) the Federal Trade Commission Act or any
8 statute defined therein as an antitrust Act;

9   (b) the Federal Food, Drug, and Cosmetic Act;

10   (c) the Hazardous Substance Act; or

11   (d) any provision of State law which would be
12 valid in the absence of such amendment unless there
13 is a direct and positive conflict between such amendment
14 in its application to interstate or foreign commerce and
15 such provision of State law.

16 EFFECTIVE DATE

17 SEC. 10. This Act shall take effect on the first day of
18 the sixth month beginning after the date of enactment of
19 this Act.

Public Law 89-755
89th Congress, S. 985
November 3, 1966

An Act

To regulate interstate and foreign commerce by preventing the use of unfair or deceptive methods of packaging or labeling of certain consumer commodities distributed in such commerce, and for other purposes.

Be it enacted by the Senate and House of Representatives of the United States of America in Congress assembled, That this Act may be cited as the "Fair Packaging and Labeling Act".

Fair Packaging
and Labeling Act.

DECLARATION OF POLICY

SEC. 2. Informed consumers are essential to the fair and efficient functioning of a free market economy. Packages and their labels should enable consumers to obtain accurate information as to the quantity of the contents and should facilitate value comparisons. Therefore, it is hereby declared to be the policy of the Congress to assist consumers and manufacturers in reaching these goals in the marketing of consumer goods.

PROHIBITION OF UNFAIR AND DECEPTIVE PACKAGING AND LABELING

SEC. 3. (a) It shall be unlawful for any person engaged in the packaging or labeling of any consumer commodity (as defined in this Act) for distribution in commerce, or for any person (other than a common carrier for hire, a contract carrier for hire, or a freight forwarder for hire) engaged in the distribution in commerce of any packaged or labeled consumer commodity, to distribute or to cause to be distributed in commerce any such commodity if such commodity is contained in a package, or if there is affixed to that commodity a label, which does not conform to the provisions of this Act and of regulations promulgated under the authority of this Act.

80 STAT. 1296
80 STAT. 1297

(b) The prohibition contained in subsection (a) shall not apply to persons engaged in business as wholesale or retail distributors of consumer commodities except to the extent that such persons (1) are engaged in the packaging or labeling of such commodities, or (2) prescribe or specify by any means the manner in which such commodities are packaged or labeled.

REQUIREMENTS AND PROHIBITIONS

SEC. 4. (a) No person subject to the prohibition contained in section 3 shall distribute or cause to be distributed in commerce any packaged consumer commodity unless in conformity with regulations which shall be established by the promulgating authority pursuant to section 6 of this Act which shall provide that—

(1) The commodity shall bear a label specifying the identity of the commodity and the name and place of business of the manufacturer, packer, or distributor;

(2) The net quantity of contents (in terms of weight, measure, or numerical count) shall be separately and accurately stated in a uniform location upon the principal display panel of that label;

(3) The separate label statement of net quantity of contents appearing upon or affixed to any package—

(A)(i) if on a package containing less than four pounds or one gallon and labeled in terms of weight or fluid measure, shall, unless subparagraph (ii) applies and such statement is set forth in accordance with such subparagraph, be expressed both in ounces (with identification as to avoirdupois or fluid ounces) and, if applicable, in pounds for weight units, with any remainder in terms of ounces or common or decimal fractions of the pound; or in the case of liquid measure, in the largest whole unit (quarts, quarts and pints, or pints, as appropriate) with any remainder in terms of fluid ounces or common or decimal fractions of the pint or quart;

(ii) if on a random package, may be expressed in terms of pounds and decimal fractions of the pound carried out to not more than two decimal places;

(iii) if on a package labeled in terms of linear measure, shall be expressed both in terms of inches and the largest whole unit (yards, yards and feet, or feet, as appropriate) with any remainder in terms of inches or common or decimal fractions of the foot or yard;

(iv) if on a package labeled in terms of measure of area, shall be expressed both in terms of square inches and the largest whole square unit (square yards, square yards and square feet, or square feet, as appropriate) with any remainder in terms of square inches or common or decimal fractions of the square foot or square yard;

(B) shall appear in conspicuous and easily legible type in distinct contrast (by typography, layout, color, embossing, or molding) with other matter on the package;

(C) shall contain letters or numerals in a type size which shall be (i) established in relationship to the area of the principal display panel of the package, and (ii) uniform for all packages of substantially the same size; and

(D) shall be so placed that the lines of printed matter included in that statement are generally parallel to the base on which the package rests as it is designed to be displayed; and

80 STAT. 1297
80 STAT. 1298

(4) The label of any package of a consumer commodity which bears a representation as to the number of servings of such commodity contained in such package shall bear a statement of the net quantity (in terms of weight, measure, or numerical count) of each such serving.

"Random package."

(5) For purposes of paragraph (3)(A)(ii) of this subsection the term "random package" means a package which is one of a lot, shipment, or delivery of packages of the same consumer commodity with varying weights, that is, packages with no fixed weight pattern.

(b) No person subject to the prohibition contained in section 3 shall distribute or cause to be distributed in commerce any packaged consumer commodity if any qualifying words or phrases appear in conjunction with the separate statement of the net quantity of contents required by subsection (a), but nothing in this subsection or in paragraph (2) of subsection (a) shall prohibit supplemental statements, at other places on the package, describing in nondeceptive terms the net quantity of contents: *Provided,* That such supplemental statements of net quantity of contents shall not include any term qualifying a unit of weight, measure, or count that tends to exaggerate the amount of the commodity contained in the package.

ADDITIONAL REGULATIONS

Sec. 5. (a) The authority to promulgate regulations under this Act is vested in (A) the Secretary of Health, Education, and Welfare (referred to hereinafter as the "Secretary") with respect to any consumer commodity which is a food, drug, device, or cosmetic, as each such term is defined by section 201 of the Federal Food, Drug, and Cosmetic Act (21 U.S.C. 321); and (B) the Federal Trade Commission (referred to hereinafter as the "Commission") with respect to any other consumer commodity.

52 Stat. 1040.

(b) If the promulgating authority specified in this section finds that, because of the nature, form, or quantity of a particular consumer commodity, or for other good and sufficient reasons, full compliance with all the requirements otherwise applicable under section 4 of this Act is impracticable or is not necessary for the adequate protection of consumers, the Secretary or the Commission (whichever the case may be) shall promulgate regulations exempting such commodity from those requirements to the extent and under such conditions as the promulgating authority determines to be consistent with section 2 of this Act.

(c) Whenever the promulgating authority determines that regulations containing prohibitions or requirements other than those prescribed by section 4 are necessary to prevent the deception of consumers or to facilitate value comparisons as to any consumer commodity, such authority shall promulgate with respect to that commodity regulations effective to—

(1) establish and define standards for characterization of the size of a package enclosing any consumer commodity, which may be used to supplement the label statement of net quantity of contents of packages containing such commodity, but this paragraph shall not be construed as authorizing any limitation on the size, shape, weight, dimensions, or number of packages which may be used to enclose any commodity; 80 STAT. 1298

(2) regulate the placement upon any package containing any commodity, or upon any label affixed to such commodity, of any printed matter stating or representing by implication that such commodity is offered for retail sale at a price lower than the ordinary and customary retail sale price or that a retail sale price advantage is accorded to purchasers thereof by reason of the size of that package or the quantity of its contents; 80 STAT. 1299

(3) require that the label on each package of a consumer commodity (other than one which is a food within the meaning of section 201(f) of the Federal Food, Drug, and Cosmetic Act) bear (A) the common or usual name of such consumer commodity, if any, and (B) in case such consumer commodity consists of two or more ingredients, the common or usual name of each such ingredient listed in order of decreasing predominance, but nothing in this paragraph shall be deemed to require that any trade secret be divulged; or 52 Stat. 1040. 21 USC 321.

(4) prevent the nonfunctional-slack-fill of packages containing consumer commodities.

For purposes of paragraph (4) of this subsection, a package shall be deemed to be nonfunctionally slack-filled if it is filled to substantially less than its capacity for reasons other than (A) protection of the contents of such package or (B) the requirements of machines used for enclosing the contents in such package.

(d) Whenever the Secretary of Commerce determines that there is undue proliferation of the weights, measures, or quantities in which any consumer commodity or reasonably comparable consumer commodities are being distributed in packages for sale at retail and such undue proliferation impairs the reasonable ability of consumers to make value comparisons with respect to such consumer commodity or commodities, he shall request manufacturers, packers, and distributors of the commodity or commodities to participate in the development of a voluntary product standard for such commodity or commodities under the procedures for the development of voluntary products standards established by the Secretary pursuant to section 2 of the Act of March 3, 1901 (31 Stat. 1449, as amended; 15 U.S.C. 272). 64 Stat. 371. Such procedures shall provide adequate manufacturer, packer, distributor, and consumer representation.

(e) If (1) after one year after the date on which the Secretary of Commerce first makes the request of manufacturers, packers, and distributors to participate in the development of a voluntary product standard as provided in subsection (d) of this section, he determines that such a standard will not be published pursuant to the provisions of such subsection (d), or (2) if such a standard is published and the Secretary of Commerce determines that it has not been observed, he shall promptly report such determination to the Congress with a statement of the efforts that have been made under the voluntary standards program and his recommendation as to whether Congress should enact legislation providing regulatory authority to deal with the situation in question.

PROCEDURE FOR PROMULGATION OF REGULATIONS

SEC. 6. (a) Regulations promulgated by the Secretary under section 4 or section 5 of this Act shall be promulgated, and shall be subject to judicial review, pursuant to the provisions of subsections (e), (f), and (g) of section 701 of the Federal Food, Drug, and Cosmetic Act (21 U.S.C. 371 (e), (f), and (g).   Hearings authorized or required for the promulgation of any such regulations by the Secretary shall be conducted by the Secretary or by such officer or employee of the Department of Health, Education, and Welfare as he may designate for that purpose.

(b) Regulations promulgated by the Commission under section 4 or section 5 of this Act shall be promulgated, and shall be subject to judicial review, by proceedings taken in conformity with the provisions of subsections (e), (f), and (g) of section 701 of the Federal Food, Drug, and Cosmetic Act (21 U.S.C. 371 (e), (f), and (g)) in the same manner, and with the same effect, as if such proceedings were taken by the Secretary pursuant to subsection (a) of this section.   Hearings authorized or required for the promulgation of any such regulations by the Commission shall be conducted by the Commission or by such officer or employee of the Commission as the Commission may designate for that purpose.

(c) In carrying into effect the provisions of this Act, the Secretary and the Commission are authorized to cooperate with any department or agency of the United States, with any State, Commonwealth, or possession of the United States, and with any department, agency, or political subdivision of any such State, Commonwealth, or possession.

(d) No regulation adopted under this Act shall preclude the continued use of returnable or reusable glass containers for beverages in inventory or with the trade as of the effective date of this Act, nor shall any regulation under this Act preclude the orderly disposal of packages in inventory or with the trade as of the effective date of such regulation.

ENFORCEMENT

SEC. 7. (a) Any consumer commodity which is a food, drug, device, or cosmetic, as each such term is defined by section 201 of the Federal Food, Drug, and Cosmetic Act (21 U.S.C. 321), and which is introduced or delivered for introduction into commerce in violation of any of the provisions of this Act, or the regulations issued pursuant to this Act, shall be deemed to be misbranded within the meaning of chapter III of the Federal Food, Drug, and Cosmetic Act, but the provisions of section 303 of that Act (21 U.S.C. 333) shall have no application to any violation of section 3 of this Act.

(b) Any violation of any of the provisions of this Act, or the regulations issued pursuant to this Act, with respect to any consumer commodity which is not a food, drug, device, or cosmetic, shall constitute

80 STAT. 1299
80 STAT. 1300

52 Stat. 1055;
70 Stat. 919.

21 USC 331-337.

an unfair or deceptive act or practice in commerce in violation of section 5(a) of the Federal Trade Commission Act and shall be subject to enforcement under section 5(b) of the Federal Trade Commission Act.

66 Stat. 632.
15 USC 45.
52 Stat. 112.

(c) In the case of any imports into the United States of any consumer commodity covered by this Act, the provisions of sections 4 and 5 of this Act shall be enforced by the Secretary of the Treasury pursuant to section 801 (a) and (b) of the Federal Food, Drug, and Cosmetic Act (21 U.S.C. 381).

52 Stat. 1058;
63 Stat. 882.

REPORTS TO THE CONGRESS

SEC. 8. Each officer or agency required or authorized by this Act to promulgate regulations for the packaging or labeling of any consumer commodity, or to participate in the development of voluntary product standards with respect to any consumer commodity under procedures referred to in section 5(d) of this Act, shall transmit to the Congress in January of each year a report containing a full and complete description of the activities of that officer or agency for the administration and enforcement of this Act during the preceding fiscal year.

80 STAT. 1300
80 STAT. 1301

COOPERATION WITH STATE AUTHORITIES

SEC. 9. (a) A copy of each regulation promulgated under this Act shall be transmitted promptly to the Secretary of Commerce, who shall (1) transmit copies thereof to all appropriate State officers and agencies, and (2) furnish to such State officers and agencies information and assistance to promote to the greatest practicable extent uniformity in State and Federal regulation of the labeling of consumer commodities.

(b) Nothing contained in this section shall be construed to impair or otherwise interfere with any program carried into effect by the Secretary of Health, Education, and Welfare under other provisions of law in cooperation with State governments or agencies, instrumentalities, or political subdivisions thereof.

DEFINITIONS

SEC. 10. For the purposes of this Act—
(a) The term "consumer commodity", except as otherwise specifically provided by this subsection, means any food, drug, device, or cosmetic (as those terms are defined by the Federal Food, Drug, and Cosmetic Act), and any other article, product, or commodity of any kind or class which is customarily produced or distributed for sale through retail sales agencies or instrumentalities for consumption by individuals, or use by individuals for purposes of personal care or in the performance of services ordinarily rendered within the household, and which usually is consumed or expended in the course of such consumption or use. Such term does not include—

21 USC 321.

(1) any meat or meat product, poultry or poultry product, or tobacco or tobacco product;
(2) any commodity subject to packaging or labeling requirements imposed by the Secretary of Agriculture pursuant to the Federal Insecticide, Fungicide, and Rodenticide Act, or the provisions of the eighth paragraph under the heading "Bureau of Animal Industry" of the Act of March 4, 1913 (37 Stat. 832-833; 21 U.S.C. 151-157), commonly known as the Virus-Serum-Toxin Act;

61 Stat. 163.
7 USC 135 note.

(3) any drug subject to the provisions of section 503(b)(1) or 506 of the Federal Food, Drug, and Cosmetic Act (21 U.S.C. 353 (b)(1) and 356);

65 Stat. 648;
55 Stat. 851.

(4) any beverage subject to or complying with packaging or labeling requirements imposed under the Federal Alcohol Administration Act (27 U.S.C. 201 et seq.) ; or

49 Stat. 977.

(5) any commodity subject to the provisions of the Federal Seed Act (7 U.S.C. 1551-1610).

53 Stat. 1275.

(b) The term "package" means any container or wrapping in which any consumer commodity is enclosed for use in the delivery or display of that consumer commodity to retail purchasers, but does not include—

(1) shipping containers or wrappings used solely for the transportation of any consumer commodity in bulk or in quantity to manufacturers, packers, or processors, or to wholesale or retail distributors thereof;

80 STAT. 1301
80 STAT. 1302

(2) shipping containers or outer wrappings used by retailers to ship or deliver any commodity to retail customers if such containers and wrappings bear no printed matter pertaining to any particular commodity; or

(3) containers subject to the provisions of the Act of August 3, 1912 (37 Stat. 250, as amended; 15 U.S.C. 231–233), the Act of March 4, 1915 (38 Stat. 1186, as amended; 15 U.S.C. 234–236), the Act of August 31, 1916 (39 Stat. 673, as amended; 15 U.S.C. 251–256), or the Act of May 21, 1928 (45 Stat. 685, as amended; 15 U.S.C. 257–257i).

(c) The term "label" means any written, printed, or graphic matter affixed to any consumer commodity or affixed to or appearing upon a package containing any consumer commodity.

(d) The term "person" includes any firm, corporation, or association.

(e) The term "commerce" means (1) commerce between any State, the District of Columbia, the Commonwealth of Puerto Rico, or any territory or possession of the United States, and any place outside thereof, and (2) commerce within the District of Columbia or within any territory or possession of the United States not organized with a legislative body, but shall not include exports to foreign countries.

(f) The term "principal display panel" means that part of a label that is most likely to be displayed, presented, shown, or examined under normal and customary conditions of display for retail sale.

SAVING PROVISION

SEC. 11. Nothing contained in this Act shall be construed to repeal, invalidate, or supersede—

38 Stat. 717.
15 USC 58.
52 Stat. 1040.
21 USC 301.
74 Stat. 372.
15 USC 1261 note.

(a) the Federal Trade Commission Act or any statute defined therein as an antitrust Act;

(b) the Federal Food, Drug, and Cosmetic Act; or

(c) the Federal Hazardous Substances Labeling Act.

EFFECT UPON STATE LAW

SEC. 12. It is hereby declared that it is the express intent of Congress to supersede any and all laws of the States or political subdivisions thereof insofar as they may now or hereafter provide for the labeling of the net quantity of contents of the package of any consumer commodity covered by this Act which are less stringent than or require information different from the requirements of section 4 of this Act or regulations promulgated pursuant thereto.

EFFECTIVE DATE

SEC. 13. This Act shall take effect on July 1, 1967: *Provided*, That the Secretary (with respect to any consumer commodity which is a

food, drug, device, or cosmetic, as those terms are defined by the Federal
Food, Drug, and Cosmetic Act), and the Commission (with respect　52 Stat. 1040.
to any other consumer commodity) may by regulation postpone, for　21 USC 321.
an additional twelve-month period, the effective date of this Act with
respect to any class or type of consumer commodity on the basis of a
finding that such a postponement would be in the public interest.

Approved November 3, 1966.

LEGISLATIVE HISTORY:

HOUSE REPORTS:　No. 2076 accompanying H. R. 15440
　　　　　　　　(Comm. on Interstate & Foreign Commerce)
　　　　　　　　and No. 2286 (Comm. of Conference).
SENATE REPORT No. 1186 (Comm. on Commerce).
CONGRESSIONAL RECORD, Vol. 112 (1966):
　　May 27, June 1, 2, 8:　Considered in Senate.
　　June 9:　Considered and passed Senate.
　　Oct. 3:　Considered and passed House, amended,
　　　　　　in lieu of H. R. 15440.
　　Oct. 17:　House agreed to conference report.
　　Oct. 19:　Senate agreed to conference report.

70
71
72
74
75
76
77
79
81
83
85
88